GoodFood

101 HEALTHY EATS
TRIPLE-TESTED RECIPES

Editor
Jane Hornby

BOOKS

Contents

GoodFood

101 HEALTHY EATS

Published in 2008 by BBC Books,
an imprint of Ebury Publishing
A Random House Group company

Copyright © Woodlands Books Ltd 2008
All photographs © BBC *Good Food*
magazine 2008
All recipes contained within this book first
appeared in BBC *Good Food* magazine

The Random House Group Limited
Reg. No. 954009

Addresses for companies within the
Random House Group can be found at
www.randomhouse.co.uk

A CIP catalogue record for this book is available
from the British Library.

The Random House Group Limited supports
The Forest Stewardship Council (FSC), the
leading international forest certification organization.
All our titles that are printed on Greenpeace
approved FSC certified paper carry the FSC logo.
Our paper procurement policy can be found at
www.rbooks.co.uk/environment

To buy books by your favourite authors and
register for offers visit www.rbooks.co.uk

Printed and bound by Firmengruppe APPL,
aprinta druck, Wemding, Germany
Colour origination by Dot Gradations Ltd, UK

Commissioning Editor: Lorna Russell
Project Editor: Laura Higginson
Designer: Annette Peppis
Production: David Brimble
Picture Researcher: Gabby Harrington

ISBN: 9781846075667

10 9 8 7 6 5 4 3 2

Introduction

At *Good Food* magazine we try to make sure that our recipes reflect the modern dilemma – we want to eat more healthily but don't want to miss out on foods we love. Each month we answer the challenge, and now we've put together 101 of our best recipes in one handy book, to make healthy eating less of a minefield.

Fancy fish and chips tonight? No problem. Think burgers are out of the question? *Good Food* has it covered. We've re-worked a range of comforting classics to make them lower in fat without compromising their flavour.

It's not just old favourites we've turned our attention to. Every recipe in this collection is low in fat, saturated fat or salt, contains one or more or your

5-a-day, is a good source of omega 3, iron or fibre – or is a superhealthy combination of all the above.

We've sorted everyday eating with a wide choice of quick, satisfying lunches, suppers and desserts, plus there are loads of light dishes for entertaining that are still big on taste. Whatever the occasion, this book should spoil you for choice, without spoiling your good intentions.

Jane Hornby
Good Food magazine

Notes and conversion tables

NOTES ON THE RECIPES
• Eggs are large in the UK and Australia and extra large in America unless stated otherwise.
• Wash fresh produce before preparation.
• Recipes contain nutritional analyses for 'sugar', which means the total sugar content including all natural sugars in the ingredients unless otherwise stated.

OVEN TEMPERATURES

Gas	°C	Fan °C	°F	Oven temp.
¼	110	90	225	Very cool
½	120	100	250	Very cool
1	140	120	275	Cool or slow
2	150	130	300	Cool or slow
3	160	140	325	Warm
4	180	160	350	Moderate
5	190	170	375	Moderately hot
6	200	180	400	Fairly hot
7	220	200	425	Hot
8	230	210	450	Very hot
9	240	220	475	Very hot

APPROXIMATE WEIGHT CONVERSIONS
• All the recipes in this book list both imperial and metric measurements. Conversions are approximate and have been rounded up or down. Follow one set of measurements only; do not mix the two.
• Cup measurements, which are used by cooks in Australia and America, have not been listed here as they vary from ingredient to ingredient. Kitchen scales should be used to measure dry/solid ingredients.
• Nutritional information does not include optional serving suggestions unless stated.

SPOON MEASURES

Spoon measurements are level unless otherwise specified.

- 1 teaspoon (tsp) = 5ml
- 1 tablespoon (tbsp) = 15ml
- 1 Australian tablespoon = 20ml (cooks in Australia should measure 3 teaspoons where 1 tablespoon is specified in a recipe)

APPROXIMATE LIQUID CONVERSIONS

metric	imperial	AUS	US
50ml	2fl oz	¼ cup	¼ cup
125ml	4fl oz	½ cup	½ cup
175ml	6fl oz	¾ cup	¾ cup
225ml	8fl oz	1 cup	1 cup
300ml	10fl oz/½ pint	½ pint	1¼ cups
450ml	16fl oz	2 cups	2 cups/1 pint
600ml	20fl oz/1 pint	1 pint	2½ cups
1 litre	35fl oz/1¾ pints	1¾ pints	1 quart

Adding extra veg to a simple burger mix keeps the meat really juicy in the middle, while also boosting your 5–a-day and making it a surprisingly low-fat option too.

Beef and salsa burgers

300g/10oz lean beef mince
50g/2oz wholemeal breadcrumbs
50g/2oz carrot, grated
1 small onion, grated
a small handful of chopped
parsley leaves
1 tsp Worcestershire sauce
4 wholemeal burger buns
salad leaves, to serve
1 small pot tomato salsa, to serve

Takes 20 minutes • Serves 4

1 Heat the grill to Medium. In a large bowl, mix together the first six ingredients, then season well. Shape the mixture into four burgers and place on a baking sheet.
2 Grill the burgers for 3–4 minutes on each side until cooked through, then keep them warm. Split each burger bun in half and place them under the grill, cut-side up, and lightly toast for 1 minute. Scatter some salad leaves over each toasted bun base, top with a burger, a good dollop of tomato salsa and the remaining bun half.

• Per serving 313 kcalories, protein 24g, carbohydrate 35g, fat 10g, saturated fat 4g, fibre 3g, sugar 5g, salt 1.99g

Adding buttermilk to mash instead of butter and milk gives it a creamy taste and texture without the saturated-fat content. This version of the classic dish is also low in salt.

Quick cottage pie

1 tbsp olive oil
500g/1lb 2oz lean minced beef
1 rasher rindless back bacon, chopped
1 onion, finely chopped
100g pack mushrooms, halved if large
1 garlic clove, finely chopped
150ml/¼ pint red wine
250ml/9fl oz beef stock (from a cube is fine)
leaves from 3 fresh thyme sprigs
1 tbsp plain flour

FOR THE TOPPING
750g/1lb 10oz potatoes, quartered
75ml/2½fl oz buttermilk or skimmed milk
2 spring onions, thinly sliced

Takes 40 minutes • Serves 4

1 Heat the oil in a non-stick frying pan, then tip in the beef and brown well, breaking up any lumps. Tip on to a plate. Add the bacon, onion, mushrooms and garlic to the pan, then cook for 5 minutes until the onion has softened.
2 Return the mince to the pan and add the wine, stock and thyme leaves. Bring to a boil, then simmer for 30 minutes or until the mince is tender. Mix the flour with a little cold water and stir into the sauce. Once thickened, tip the mix into a medium-sized ovenproof dish. Preheat the oven to 220°C/fan 200°C/Gas 7.
3 Meanwhile, cook the potatoes in a pan of boiling water for 15 minutes until soft. Drain and mash with the buttermilk, then stir in half the spring onions. Spoon the mash over the mince and fluff up. Bake in the oven for 15 minutes until lightly browned. Serve sprinkled with the remaining spring onions.

• Per serving 390 kcalories, protein 36g, carbohydrate 40g, fat 11g, saturated fat 3g, fibre 3g, sugar 5g, salt 0.8g

Curries don't need masses of fat, as this delicious recipe that's low in fat and saturated fat amply proves. Frying the spices first enhances their flavour, while yogurt gives the dish all the creaminess you need.

Aromatic chicken curry

3 tbsp sunflower oil
6 skinless chicken thighs, on the bone
1 onion, chopped
5 bay leaves
2 cinnamon sticks
6 cardamon pods, lightly crushed
250ml/9fl oz Greek yogurt
20g pack fresh coriander, leaves and stems chopped
4 tbsp korma curry paste
85g/3oz sultanas
naan bread and mango chutney, to serve (optional)

Takes 50 minutes • Serves 6

1 Preheat the oven to 180°C/fan 160°C/ Gas 4. Heat one tablespoon of the oil in a large casserole dish with a lid. Add the chicken and cook for about 7–10 minutes or until golden all over, then remove from the pan and set aside. Fry the onion with the bay leaves and the spices in the remaining oil for about 5 minutes, until soft and golden. Take off the heat and return the chicken to the pan.
2 Mix the yogurt, coriander, curry paste and sultanas together, pour over the chicken and give it a stir. Cover with the lid and cook in the oven for 30 minutes, or until the meat falls off the bone easily. Serve with naans and mango chutney.

• Per serving 217 kcalories, protein 23g, carbohydrate 13g, fat 9g, saturated fat 3g, fibre 1g, sugar 12g, salt 0.68g

Yes, even comforting toad-in-the-hole can be healthy and low in fat! If you prefer, swap the apple for a large onion.

Sausage and apple toad

1 tbsp sunflower oil
4 half-fat sausages
50g/2oz plain flour
150ml/¼pint skimmed milk
2 tsp wholegrain mustard
1 egg
1 eating apple, quartered, cored and sliced

Takes 30 minutes • Serves 4

1 Preheat the oven to 240°C/fan 220°C/ Gas 9. Brush a four-hole Yorkshire pudding tin with the oil, then place a sausage in each dip. Cook the sausages in the tin set over a high heat for 5 minutes or until browned.

2 Tip the flour into a bowl, season and make a well in the centre. Whisk the milk, mustard and egg together, then pour a third of the mix into the well. Gradually draw the flour into the milk to form a paste. Whisk in the rest of the milk mix to make a smooth batter.

3 While still over the heat, cut each of the sausages in half using a pair of kitchen scissors. Scatter the apple slices among the four sausages in their dips. Pour the batter over. Take off the heat and bake in the oven for 20 minutes until risen and golden. Serve with mashed potato, peas and gravy.

• Per toad 221 kcalories, protein 12g, carbohydrate 20g, fat 11g, saturated fat 3g, fibre 2g, sugar 7g, salt 1.43g

Buying lean mince is a simple way to reduce your fat intake without effort, so this rich and tasty bolognese is low in fat and as a bonus provides two of your 5-a-day.

Speedy pasta bolognese

500g pack lean beef mince (no more than 5% fat)
a handful of mushrooms, sliced
2 garlic cloves, crushed
3 tbsp sun-dried tomato purée
400g can chopped tomatoes
1 glass red wine or 150ml/¼ pint beef stock
1 tsp dried mixed herbs
400g/14oz penne
a handful of basil leaves, torn, to serve

Takes 25 minutes • Serves 4

1 Without adding any extra fat, brown the beef in a large frying pan for 5 minutes then throw in the mushrooms and cook for 3 minutes to soften. Stir in the garlic and sun-dried tomato purée and cook for 2 minutes. Add the tomatoes, wine or stock, dried herbs and some seasoning. Bring to the boil, then simmer for 10 minutes.
2 While the sauce is simmering, cook the pasta according to the packet instructions, drain, then serve with the sauce and torn basil leaves scattered on top.

• Per serving 574 kcalories, protein 41g, carbohydrate 81g, fat 11g, saturated fat 3g, fibre 4g, sugar 6g, salt 0.56g

This take-away classic can easily be made healthy, yet remain just as delicious as the original, when you know how. This low-fat version is also high in fibre, folic acid and vitamin C.

Fish, chips and mushy peas

400g/14oz baking potatoes
2 tsp olive oil
2 slices white bread
2 white fish fillets
1 tbsp plain flour, seasoned
1 egg, beaten
140g/5oz frozen peas with mint
2 tbsp half-fat crème fraîche

Takes 50 minutes • Serves 2

1 Preheat the oven to 200°C/fan 180°C/ Gas 6. Peel the potatoes, cut into thick chips, then toss with the olive oil and a little salt. Arrange them on a large, non-stick baking sheet and roast for 20 minutes, turning halfway through.
2 Lightly toast the bread, then pulse briefly in a food processor to make coarse breadcrumbs. Dust the fish in flour, shaking off the excess, then dip it first into the egg and then the breadcrumbs, and coat thoroughly. Roast the fish with the chips for a further 20 minutes or until both are golden.
3 Just before the fish and chips are ready, boil the peas for 3–4 minutes, then drain and mash. Stir in the crème fraîche, and season.

• Per serving 484 kcalories, protein 42g, carbohydrate 58g, fat 11g, saturated fat 3g, fibre 6g, sugar 4g, salt 1.09g

These kebabs are packed with flavour instead of fat, and the minty yogurt sauce is a good source of calcium. Try making them with chicken for an even leaner version.

Minty lamb kebabs

150ml pot natural yogurt
1½ tbsp mint sauce
1 tsp ground cumin
300g/10oz diced lean lamb
½ small onion, cut into large chunks
2 large pitta breads
2 large handfuls of lettuce, shredded

Takes 30 minutes • Serves 2

1 Heat the grill to Medium. In a bowl, mix the yogurt and mint sauce together, then divide the mixture in half. Stir the cumin into one half of the yogurt mix, then add the diced lamb and mix thoroughly to coat and season well.
2 Thread the lamb on to four skewers, alternating each chunk with pieces of onion, then arrange the skewers on the wire rack of a grill pan. Grill the kebabs for 3–4 minutes on each side or until the lamb is cooked through and the onion is beginning to brown.
3 Warm the pittas for 1–2 minutes in a toaster then split them open. Stuff the pittas with the lamb, onion and some lettuce, drizzling over the remaining minty yogurt sauce, to serve.

• Per serving 538 kcalories, protein 43g, carbohydrate 62g, fat 15g, saturated fat 7g, fibre 3g, sugar 11g, salt 1.68g

Spices have a natural affinity with smoked haddock – just think of kedgeree. This filling, creamy bowlful makes a great low-fat lunch or supper served with crusty bread.

Smoked haddock and cumin chowder

400g/14oz undyed smoked
haddock fillets
a few black peppercorns
1 bay leaf
500ml/16fl oz semi-skimmed milk
700ml/1¼ pints fish, vegetable or
chicken stock
25g/1oz butter
4 leeks, trimmed, washed and thinly
sliced into rings
½ tsp cumin seeds
4 medium potatoes, cut into chunks

Takes 25 minutes • Serves 4

1 Put the peppercorns and bay leaf into a shallow pan, add the fish, skin-side down, then cover with the milk and stock. Bring to a very gentle simmer, then poach the fish for 5–8 minutes, until it just starts to flake at the thickest part. Carefully lift out the fish and set aside.

2 Meanwhile, heat the butter in a large pan, then soften the leeks for 10 minutes without colouring. Once soft, turn up the heat a little and add the cumin seeds, frying them until they sizzle and start to smell toasty. Tip in the potatoes, then add the poaching liquid and simmer for 20 minutes until the potatoes are tender and starting to fall apart. Just before serving, flake the fish and stir through. Spoon into shallow bowls and serve.

• Per serving 314 kcalories, protein 28g, carbohydrate 32g, fat 9g, saturated fat 5g, fibre 5g, sugar 10g, salt 2.14g

If you're counting the calories but love Chinese food, make your own guilt-free, low-fat Chinese chicken with vitamin-C boosting veg. Delicious served hot from the wok with steaming rice.

Chinese chicken

1 egg white
1 tbsp cornflour, plus 1 tsp extra
4 boneless, skinless chicken breasts, sliced
1–2 tbsp vegetable oil
1 tbsp fish sauce
juice of 1 lime
1 red pepper, seeded and cut into large chunks
a thumb-size knob of fresh root ginger, grated
1 shallot, thinly sliced
1 garlic clove, thinly sliced
1 red chilli, seeded and sliced (optional)
a handful of fresh basil leaves
boiled rice, to serve

Takes 30 minutes, plus marinating
Serves 4

1 Beat together the egg white and one tablespoon of cornflour in a bowl. Tip in the chicken and coat with the mix. Marinate for 15 minutes at room temperature.
2 Remove the chicken from the egg marinade and pat dry with kitchen paper. Heat a wok and pour in one tablespoon of oil. Cook the chicken for 5–7 minutes, tossing until just cooked. Set aside. Meanwhile, combine the fish sauce, lime juice, 55ml/2fl oz water and the extra teaspoon of cornflour.
3 Add a little more oil to the pan if you need to, and stir fry the pepper for 1 minute, then tip in the ginger, shallot, garlic and chilli, if using, and fry for 1–2 minutes more. Tip the fish-sauce mix into the wok, then add the chicken. Heat through, then stir in the basil and serve with boiled rice.

• Per serving 501 kcalories, protein 42g, carbohydrate 76g, fat 5g, saturated fat 1g, fibre 2g, sugar 3g, salt 1.02g

Lean pork is low in saturated fat, making it a brilliantly healthy choice.
Serve tasty schnitzels with crisp homemade coleslaw and you'll get one
of your 5-a-day from this superhealthy supper.

Crisp pork schnitzels

4 × 175g/6oz pork loin steaks,
fat trimmed
2 slices white bread
a handful of fresh sage leaves
25g/1oz Parmesan, finely grated
1 egg, beaten
1 tbsp oil
lemon wedges, to serve (optional)

FOR THE COLESLAW
½ white cabbage, core removed,
finely shredded
4 tbsp buttermilk or low-fat
natural yogurt
2 red-skinned eating apples, halved
and sliced

Takes 30 minutes • Serves 4

1 Lay the pork steaks between two sheets of cling film or baking paper and bash with a rolling pin until they are approximately 1cm/½ in thick. Whiz the bread in a food processor to make breadcrumbs. Add the sage and pulse a few times to chop the leaves roughly. Mix in the Parmesan and spread the mixture over a large plate. Season with black pepper.
2 One by one, dip each pork steak into the beaten egg, allow the excess to drip off, then press the meat into the breadcrumb mix on both sides. Set aside. Heat the oil in a large non-stick frying pan and fry the steaks for 3–4 minutes each side until cooked through.
3 Meanwhile, combine the cabbage, buttermilk or yogurt and apple slices, then season. Serve the steaks with the coleslaw and a lemon wedge, if using, for squeezing over the pork.

• Per serving 380 kcalories, protein 47g, carbohydrate 21g, fat 13g, saturated fat 4g, fibre 3g, sugar 12g, salt 0.7g

There's no need for coconut milk or cream in this clever korma – ground almonds enrich the sauce beautifully. This tasty curry is low in fat, saturated fat and salt.

Quick prawn korma

1 tbsp sunflower oil
1 onion, chopped
400g pack frozen raw peeled prawns, defrosted
2 tbsp korma curry paste
3 tbsp ground almonds
a handful of fresh coriander leaves, roughly chopped
boiled rice, to serve (optional)

Takes 15 minutes, plus desfrosting
Serves 4

1 Heat the oil in a frying pan, add the onion, then fry for 5 minutes until lightly coloured. Add the prawns, then stir quickly until they are evenly pink. Stir in the curry paste and add 150ml/¼ pint water and the ground almonds. Bring to the boil, then simmer for 2–3 minutes or until the sauce has thickened slightly. Scatter with the chopped coriander and serve with boiled rice.

• Per serving 188 kcalories, protein 21g, carbohydrate 4g, fat 10g, saturated fat 1g, fibre 1g, sugar 2g, salt 0.8g

This low-fat, warming one-pot is full of flavour and provides one of your 5-a-day. Serve it with a simple salad to boost the veg content.

Tasty chicken tagine

2 tbsp olive oil
8 boneless skinless chicken thighs, halved if large
1 onion, chopped
2 tsp fresh root ginger grated
a pinch of saffron or turmeric
1 tbsp clear honey
400g/14oz carrots, cut into sticks
one small bunch parsley, roughly chopped
lemon wedges, to serve

Takes 50 minutes • Serves 4

1 Heat the oil in a large, wide pan with a lid, add the chicken and fry, uncovered, until lightly coloured. Add the onion and ginger, then fry for a further 2 minutes. Add 150ml/¼ pint water, the saffron, honey and carrots, season, then stir well.
2 Bring to the boil, cover tightly, then simmer for 30 minutes or until the chicken is tender. Remove the lid and increase the heat for about 5 minutes to reduce the sauce a little. Sprinkle with parsley and serve with lemon wedges for squeezing over.

• Per serving 304 kcalories, protein 39g, carbohydrate 14g, fat 11g, saturated fat 3g, fibre 3g, sugar 12g, salt 0.48g

There's no reason to say no to noodles with this low-fat classic.

Pad Thai in four easy steps

250g pack medium rice noodles
2 tsp tamarind paste
3 tbsp fish sauce
2 tsp sugar
2 tbsp vegetable oil
1 garlic clove, chopped
3 spring onions, sliced
1 egg
200g pack large cooked prawns
75g/3oz beansprouts
a handful of salted peanuts,
chopped, to serve
lime wedges, to serve

Takes 25 minutes • Serves 4

1 Tip the noodles into a bowl and pour over boiling water until they are covered. Leave to stand for 5–10 minutes until the noodles are soft, then drain well. Mix together the tamarind paste, fish sauce and sugar.
2 Heat a wok or large frying pan over a high heat. Swirl in the oil then tip in the garlic and spring onions. Stir fry for 30 seconds, until they just begin to soften.
3 Push the vegetables to the sides of the wok, then crack the egg into the centre. Keep stirring the egg for 30 seconds until it begins to set and resembles a broken-up omelette.
4 Add the prawns and beansprouts, then the noodles. Pour over the fish-sauce mixture, toss everything together and heat through. Spoon on to plates and serve with sprinkled chopped peanuts and lime wedges.

• Per serving 359 kcalories, protein 19g, carbohydrate 57g, fat 8g, saturated fat 1g, fibre 1g, sugar 5g, salt 3.17g

It's amazing what you can make with just a few ingredients in the house – this one-pan recipe is low in fat, speedy and saves on the washing up.

Healthy egg and chips

500g/1lb 2oz potatoes, diced
2 shallots, sliced
1 tbsp olive oil
2 tsp dried oregano or 1 tsp fresh leaves
200g/8oz small mushrooms
4 eggs

Takes 40 minutes • Serves 4

1 Preheat the oven to 200°C/fan 180°C/Gas 6. Tip the potatoes and shallots into a large, non-stick roasting tin, drizzle with the oil, sprinkle over the oregano, then mix everything together well. Bake in the oven for 15 minutes, add the mushrooms, then cook for a further 10 minutes until the potatoes are browned and tender.

2 Make four gaps in the vegetables then crack an egg into each space. Return to the oven for 3–4 minutes or until the eggs are cooked to your liking.

• Per serving 218 kcalories, protein 11g, carbohydrate 22g, fat 10g, saturated fat 2g, fibre 2g, sugar 1g, salt 0.24g

Get your 5-a-day quota all in one portion of this hearty ricotta and spinach lasagne.

Five-veg lasagne

4 tbsp olive oil
1 large aubergine, cut into small cubes
350g/12oz mushrooms, chopped
4 roasted red peppers, chopped
700g jar passata with onions and garlic
8–10 dried lasagne sheets
400g/14oz frozen spinach, defrosted
250g tub ricotta
25g/1oz grated parmesan
25g/1oz pine nuts

Takes 55 minutes, plus defrosting
Serves 4

1 Preheat the oven to 180°C/fan 160°C/ Gas 4. Heat two tablespoons of oil in a non-stick frying pan. Fry the aubergine for 5 minutes until softened, then tip into a bowl. Fry the mushrooms in the remaining oil for a few minutes until golden, then mix with the aubergine and add the peppers.
2 Put half the vegetables into a 20x30cm/ 8x12in baking dish. Spoon over half the passata, cover with lasagne sheets. Spread the rest of the veg over the pasta, cover with passata then pasta. Drain any excess liquid from the spinach and mix with the ricotta and half the Parmesan. Spoon over the pasta, then sprinkle with the remaining Parmesan and pine nuts. Cover with foil, bake for 20 minutes, uncover, then bake for another 10 minutes until browned. Serve with green salad.

• Per serving 528 kcalories, protein 21g, carbohydrate 46g, fat 30g, saturated fat 8g, fibre 9g, sugar 13g, salt 2.11g

Hoisin sauce, much like soy sauce, adds loads of flavour without fat. These wraps are the perfect choice for lunchboxes as there's no lettuce to go soggy.

Chicken hoisin wraps

2 flour tortillas
4 tsp hoisin sauce
100g/4oz leftover chicken breast, shredded
¼ cucumber, cut into thin sticks
2 spring onions, shredded

Takes 10 minutes • Serves 2

1 Warm the tortillas in a hot, dry pan or in the microwave for a few seconds.
2 Spread each tortilla thinly with two teaspoons of the hoisin sauce, then scatter over the cooked chicken, cucumber sticks and spring onion. Wrap tightly and enjoy.

• Per wrap 222 kcalories, protein 19.4g, carbohydrate 27.2g, fat 4.7g, saturated fat 1.2g, fibre 1.3g, sugar 5.2g, salt 1.68g

Much more subtle than the standard Kiev, this easy one-pan recipe is lower in fat, too.

Easy chicken Kievs

4 boneless, skinless chicken breasts
25g/1oz garlic butter, softened
25g/1oz breadcrumbs

Takes 25 minutes • Serves 4

1 Place the chicken on a baking sheet, rub with a little of the butter, season and cook under the grill on a medium heat for 15 minutes, turning once, until cooked through.
2 Mix together the remaining garlic butter and breadcrumbs. Remove the chicken from the grill and top each breast with a smear of the breadcrumbed butter. Return to the grill for 3–5 minutes more, until the breadcrumbs are golden and the butter melted. Serve the kievs with their buttery juices, alongside new potatoes and peas or broad beans.

• Per kiev 218 kcalories, protein 34g, carbohydrate 5g, fat 7g, saturated fat 4g, fibre none, sugar none, salt 0.37g

Pork fillet is very low in fat, and so can be easily overcooked – adding the just undercooked pork to the sauce a few minutes before serving finishes the cooking and helps to keep the meat juicy.

Spicy sweet and sour pork

2 tbsp vegetable or sunflower oil
400g/14oz pork fillet (tenderloin), cut into thick slices
1 onion, cut into chunks
200g can pineapple chunks in syrup, drained, and syrup reserved
1 tbsp tomato ketchup
½ × 400g can chopped plum tomatoes
150ml/¼ pint chicken stock
1 tsp cornflour
1 cinnamon stick
boiled rice, to serve (optional)

Takes 25 minutes • Serves 4

1 Heat one tablespoon of oil in a large, deep frying pan and fry the pork for 5 minutes until golden, but not completely cooked through. Take the meat out of the pan and set aside.
2 Heat another tablespoon of oil in the pan and add the onion, frying for 5 minutes until it starts to soften. Tip in the pineapple, along with three tablespoons of the syrup, the ketchup, tomatoes, stock and cinnamon stick. Bring to the boil, then simmer for 10 minutes or until the sauce has thickened slightly.
3 Add the pork to the sauce in the pan and simmer for another 4 minutes. Mix the cornflour with a little cold water, add to the sauce and stir until thickened. Serve with rice.

• Per serving 213 kcalories, protein 23g, carbohydrate 13g, fat 8g, saturated fat 3g, fibre 1g, sugar 11g, salt 0.52g

There's so much creaminess in the grains of risotto rice, you don't need to add fat. The butternut squash is a good source of vitamin C and gives you one of your 5-a-day.

Butternut squash risotto

250g/9oz risotto rice
700ml/1¼ pint hot vegetable stock
1 medium butternut squash
a big handful of grated Parmesan,
plus extra to serve
a handful of fresh sage leaves,
roughly chopped

Takes 25 minutes • Serves 4

1 Tip the rice into a large bowl, then add 500ml/¾ pint of the hot vegetable stock. Cover with cling film and microwave on High for 5 minutes. Meanwhile, peel, seed and cut the squash into medium chunks. Stir the rice, then add the squash and the rest of the stock.

2 Re-cover with cling film, then microwave for another 15 minutes, stirring halfway, until almost all the stock is absorbed, and the rice and squash are tender.

3 Leave the risotto to sit for 2 minutes, then stir in the Parmesan and sage. Serve topped with more grated cheese.

• Per serving 313 kcalories, protein 10g, carbohydrate 66g, fat 3g, saturated fat 1g, fibre 4g, sugar 9g, salt 1.04g

Parmesan sizzles around skinless chicken to make a deliciously savoury yet low-fat dish that's packed with vitamin C.

Parmesan spring chicken

1 egg white
5 tbsp finely grated Parmesan
4 boneless skinless chicken breasts
400g/14oz new potatoes, cut into small cubes
140g/5oz frozen peas
a good handful of baby spinach leaves
1 tbsp white wine vinegar
2 tbsp olive oil

Takes 20 minutes • Serves 4

1 Heat the grill to Medium and line the grill pan with foil. Beat the egg white in a flattish bowl with a little salt and pepper. Tip the Parmesan on to a plate. Dip the chicken first in the egg white, then in the cheese. Grill the coated chicken for 10–12 minutes until browned and crisp, turning once halfway through cooking.

2 Meanwhile, boil the potatoes for 10 minutes, adding the peas for the final 3 minutes, then drain. Toss the vegetables with the spinach leaves, vinegar and oil, and add seasoning to taste. Divide among four warm plates, then serve with the chicken.

• Per serving 339 kcalories, protein 42g, carbohydrate 20g, fat 11g, saturated fat 3g, fibre 3g, sugar 3g, salt 0.53g

Mackerel goes perfectly with curry spices and salsa. This filling dish is low in salt, a good source of omega-3 and provides one of your 5-a-day.

Spiced mackerel on toast with beetroot salsa

4 mackerel fillets, halved widthways
olive oil, for drizzling
1 tsp mild curry powder
4 slices from a sourdough loaf or ciabatta

FOR THE SALSA
250g pack beetroot (not in vinegar), diced
1 eating apple, cut into wedges then thinly sliced
1 small red onion, finely sliced
juice of ½ lemon
1 tbsp olive oil
1 tsp cumin seeds
1 small bunch coriander, leaves roughly chopped

Takes 15 minutes • Serves 4

1 For the salsa, mix the beetroot, apple, onion, lemon juice, oil, cumin and coriander together, season well, then set aside while you cook the mackerel.

2 Heat the grill to High. Put the fish on to a sheet of foil laid over the grill rack, sprinkle over the curry powder, drizzle with oil, then season and rub the oil and spice mix well into the fish. Grill for 4–5 minutes until the skin is crisp and the fillets are cooked through; you won't need to turn the fish over.

3 Toast the bread in a toaster or alongside the fish under the grill, then drizzle with a little olive oil. Top with the salsa and mackerel, then pour over any pan juices and eat straight away.

• Per serving 471 kcalories, protein 25g, carbohydrate 35g, fat 27g, saturated fat 5g, fibre 3g, sugar 11g, salt 0.97g

A tasty sauce made with storecupboard ingredients transforms pork fillet into something special, yet still low in salt and saturated fat.

Sticky maple pork with apples

600g/1lb 5oz pork fillet
1 tbsp olive oil
2 eating apples, cored and cut into eighths
1 garlic clove, crushed
2 tbsp maple syrup
1 tbsp white wine vinegar
2 tbsp wholegrain mustard
rice, to serve (optional)

Takes 20 minutes • Serves 4

1 Cut the pork into slices 3cm/1in thick. Heat the oil in a large, non-stick frying pan, add the pork, then fry on both sides until lightly browned, about 5 minutes in total. Lift out of the pan and set aside. Add the apples to the pan and cook them for 3–4 minutes or until starting to soften.
2 Stir in the garlic, maple syrup, vinegar and three tablespoons of water, bring to the boil, then return the meat to the pan along with any juices. Simmer for a few more minutes, stirring until the pork is cooked through and the sauce is thick and sticky. Stir in the wholegrain mustard and serve.

• Per serving 303 kcalories, protein 34g, carbohydrate 13g, fat 13g, saturated fat 4g, fibre 1g, sugar 12g, salt 0.52g

Unlike most Tex-Mex dishes, these fish fillets are low in saturated fat and salt. Serve with fluffy rice, tacos or toasted tortillas to make them an inspired change from chicken fajitas.

Tex-Mex fish fillets

4 boneless white fish fillets, about 140g/5oz each
2 tbsp fajita or Tex-Mex seasoning
2 tbsp sunflower oil
200g pot guacamole
a handful of fresh coriander leaves, roughly chopped
lime wedges, to serve

Takes 15 minutes • Serves 4

1 Dust the fish in the seasoning, then set aside. Heat the oil in a shallow frying pan, then fry the fish for 3–4 minutes on each side until crisp.

2 Serve each piece of fish with a spoonful of guacamole on top, a scattering of chopped coriander and a lime wedge for squeezing.

• Per serving 245 kcalories, protein 27g, carbohydrate 2g, fat 14g, saturated fat 2g, fibre 1g, sugar 1g, salt 0.54g

Lentils should be an essential ingredient in your storecupboard – they're a versatile source of protein and great value. This smart dish is superhealthy: low in saturated fat and a good source of omega 3.

Salmon with leeks and lentils

2 leeks, trimmed, washed and each cut into about 5 chunks
2 skinless salmon fillets, each about 100g/4oz
410g can green lentils, drained and rinsed under hot water
4 tbsp low-fat vinaigrette dressing
2 handfuls of baby spinach leaves

Takes 20 minutes • Serves 2

1 Steam the leeks for 10 minutes until soft, then lay the salmon on top and continue to steam for 5 minutes or until the salmon is cooked through.

2 While the salmon and leeks are steaming, tip the lentils into a bowl with most of the dressing and some seasoning. When the salmon is cooked, lift it out of the steamer and set aside. Tip the leeks in with the lentils, add the baby spinach leaves and toss well. Divide the lentil salad between two plates, top with the fish and drizzle over the remaining dressing.

• Per serving 322 kcalories, protein 32g, carbohydrate 21g, fat 13g, saturated fat 2g, fibre 7g, sugar 5g, salt 2.02g

A zesty, light and summery dish that's low in saturated fat and salt. If you have time, marinade the chicken in the fridge for up to a day while the flavours work their magic.

Chargrilled lime chicken

4 boneless chicken breasts, skin on
1 tsp black peppercorns
3cm/1in fresh root ginger
2 garlic cloves
1 tbsp soy sauce
zest of 1 and juice of 2 limes, plus lime wedges to serve

Takes 30 minutes, plus 10 minutes marinating • Serves 4

1 Slash each chicken breast three times and put them in a shallow dish. Crush the peppercorns coarsely in a mortar. Finely grate the ginger, crush the garlic and mix with the peppercorns, soy sauce, and lime zest and juice. Mix well, then pour over the chicken and leave to marinate in the fridge for at least 10 minutes, or overnight.

2 Heat a grill or griddle pan, then cook the chicken for 6–8 minutes on each side until cooked through. Alternatively, you could cook this on the barbecue: cook for the same length of time, but make sure the coals are not too fierce. Transfer to a serving dish, then carefully pour over any cooking juices. Serve with wedges of lime for squeezing.

• Per serving 225 kcalories, protein 37g, carbohydrate 2g, fat 8g, saturated fat 2g, fibre none, sugar 1g, salt 0.87g

Perk up pasta with a simple, low-fat sauce that's packed with flavour and gives you two of your 5-a-day.

Spicy spaghetti with garlic mushrooms

2 tbsp olive oil
250g pack chestnut mushrooms, thickly sliced
1 garlic clove, thinly sliced
1 small bunch parsley, leaves only
1 onion, finely chopped
1 celery stick, finely chopped
400g can chopped tomatoes
½ red chilli, seeded and finely chopped (or use dried chilli flakes)
300g/10oz spaghetti

Takes 25 minutes • Serves 4

1 Heat one tablespoon of the oil in a pan, add the mushrooms, then fry over a high heat for 3 minutes until golden and softened. Add the garlic, fry for 1 minute more, then tip into a bowl with the parsley and set aside.
2 Add the onion and celery to the pan with the rest of the oil, then fry for 5 minutes until lightly coloured. Stir in the tomatoes, chilli and a little salt, then bring to the boil. Reduce the heat and simmer, uncovered, for 10 minutes until thickened.
3 Meanwhile, boil the spaghetti according to the packet instructions, then drain. Toss with the sauce, top with the garlicky mushrooms, then serve.

• Per serving 346 kcalories, protein 12g, carbohydrate 62g, fat 7g, saturated fat 1g, fibre 5g, sugar 7g, salt 0.35g

A succulent low-fat, low-salt pork supper that's on the table in only 15 minutes. Delicious served with mash or boiled potatoes to soak up the juices.

Clementine pork steaks

2 tbsp sunflower oil
4 lean pork steaks, about
100g/4oz each
200g/8oz mushrooms, sliced
2 tsp paprika
2 tbsp redcurrant jelly
50ml/2fl oz clementine juice (from
about 2 clementines)
1 tbsp red wine vinegar

Takes 15 minutes • Serves 4

1 Heat one tablespoon of the oil in a frying pan, add the pork steaks and fry quickly until browned on both sides (the steaks will still be underdone in the middle at this point). Remove from the pan, add the remaining oil, then fry the mushrooms until softened.
2 Return the pork to the pan, sprinkle in the paprika and stir in the redcurrant jelly, clementine juice and red wine vinegar. Bring to the boil, stirring to dissolve the jelly. Simmer for about 5 minutes, turning the pork halfway through, until the meat and mushrooms are tender.

• Per serving 207 kcalories, protein 24g, carbohydrate 7g, fat 10g, saturated fat 2g, fibre 1g, sugar 6g, salt 0.17g

Steaming is one of the healthiest ways to cook – this recipe has bags of flavour but less than 200 calories per serving. It is also a good source of omega-3 and provides one of your 5-a-day.

Chinese steamed bass with greens

2 sustainable bass or other white fish fillets, about 100g/4oz each
1 red or green chilli, seeded and finely chopped
1 tsp fresh root ginger, finely chopped
300g/10oz green cabbage or other greens, finely shredded
2 tsp sunflower oil
1 tsp sesame oil
2 garlic cloves, thinly sliced
2 tsp low-salt soy sauce

Takes 20 minutes • Serves 2

1 Sprinkle the fish with the chilli, ginger and a little salt. Steam the cabbage for 5 minutes. Lay the fish on top of the cabbage and steam for a further 5 minutes or until cooked through.
2 Meanwhile, heat the oils in a small pan, add the garlic and quickly cook, stirring until lightly browned. Transfer the cabbage and fish to serving plates, sprinkle each with one teaspoon of soy sauce, then pour over the garlicky oil.

• Per serving 188 kcalories, protein 23g, carbohydrate 8g, fat 8g, saturated fat 1g, fibre 4g, sugar 7g, salt 0.74g

Cooking the rice and chicken with the lid on keeps all the flavours sealed in. This tasty one-pot is a good source of iron and vitamin C, provides two of your 5-a-day and is low in fat, saturated fat and salt.

Lemon chicken and cauliflower pilaf

4 boneless, chicken breasts, skin on
1 tbsp medium curry powder (one with turmeric in it)
200g/8oz basmati rice
500ml/18fl oz chicken stock
200g/8oz cauliflower florets
200g/8oz frozen green beans
1 lemon, halved lengthways and sliced
1 small bunch coriander, leaves and stalks separated and roughly chopped

Takes 20 minutes • Serves 4

1 Heat a large frying pan or flameproof casserole, then brown the chicken, skin-side down. Tip in the curry powder and rice, fry for 1 minute, then stir in the stock.
2 Add the cauliflower, beans, lemon slices and coriander stalks to the pan, and turn the chicken skin-side up. Bring to the boil, then simmer with the lid on for 10 minutes or until the chicken is cooked through and the rice is tender. Season to taste, sprinkle over the coriander leaves and serve.

• Per serving 360 kcalories, protein 41g, carbohydrate 45g, fat 3g, saturated fat 1g, fibre 3g, sugar 3g, salt 0.77g

Bold flavours make this stew perfect comfort food for a winter night. It's low in saturated fat and salt and a good source of vitamin C. Add a splash of wine if you've got a bottle open and serve with polenta.

Italian-style beef stew

1 onion, sliced
1 garlic clove, sliced
2 tbsp olive oil
300g/10oz beef steak, thinly sliced
1 yellow pepper, seeded and thinly sliced
400g can chopped tomatoes
1 fresh rosemary sprig, leaves chopped
1 handful of pitted black olives

Takes 30 minutes • Serves 4

1 In a large pan, fry the beef strips in oil for 2 minutes until browned. Tip the beef out, then add the onion and garlic, and fry for 5 minutes until softened. Add the pepper, tomatoes and rosemary to the pan, then bring to the boil. Simmer for 15 minutes until reduced.
2 Stir through the beef strips and olives, cook for a further 2 minutes then serve.

• Per serving 225 kcalories, protein 25g, carbohydrate 7g, fat 11g, saturated fat 3g, fibre 2g, sugar 6g, salt 0.87g

Pick up a few items from the deli counter and this light Mediterranean pasta can be ready in no time. Low in saturated fat and salt, this dish will set you up for summer.

Artichoke, olive and lemon pasta

400g/14oz spaghetti
zest and juice of 1 lemon
3 tbsp olive oil
50g/2oz freshly grated Parmesan
100g/4oz artichoke hearts from a jar, chopped if large
a handful of black olives
100g bag wild rocket

Takes 15 minutes • Serves 4

1 Cook the pasta in a large pan of boiling water according to the packet instructions.
2 While it cooks, mix together the lemon zest and juice, oil and Parmesan. Drain the pasta, reserving three tablespoons of the cooking water, then return to the pan with the lemon mix, cooking water, artichokes and olives. Heat through briefly, season well, stir through the rocket, then serve.

• Per serving 528 kcalories, protein 18g, carbohydrate 76g, fat 19g, saturated fat 4g, fibre 4g, sugar 4g, salt 1.05g

A light, fragrant low-fat twist on classic curry. It makes a great lunchbox filler cold, is a good source of iron and provides two of your 5-a-day.

Spiced chicken with rice and crisp red onions

2 boneless, skinless chicken breasts, about 140g/5oz each
1 tbsp sunflower oil
2 tsp curry powder
1 large red onion, thinly sliced
100g/4oz basmati rice
1 cinnamon stick
a pinch of saffron
1 tbsp raisins
85g/3oz frozen peas
1 tbsp each chopped fresh mint and coriander leaves
4 rounded tbsp low-fat natural yogurt

Takes 35 minutes • Serves 2

1 Preheat the oven to 190°C/fan 170°C/ Gas 5. Brush the chicken with one teaspoon of oil, then sprinkle with curry powder. Toss the onion in the remaining oil. Put the chicken and onions in one layer in a roasting tin. Bake for 25 minutes until the meat is cooked and the onions are crisp, stirring the onions halfway through the cooking time.
2 Rinse the rice, then put in a pan with the cinnamon, saffron, salt to taste and 300ml/ ½ pint water. Bring to the boil, stir once, add the raisins, then cover. Gently cook for 10–12 minutes until the rice is tender, adding the peas halfway through. Spoon the rice on to two plates, top with the chicken and scatter over the onions. Stir the herbs into the yogurt and season, if you like, before serving on the side.

• Per serving 495 kcalories, protein 45g, carbohydrate 63g, fat 9g, saturated fat 2g, fibre 5g, sugar 15g, salt 0.39g

Garlicky lamb and spices come together on crisp bread to make a low-fat Turkish twist on pizza. This is delicious served with a tomato and cucumber salad.

Fragrant lamb flatbreads

½ × 500g pack bread mix
1 onion, finely chopped
250g/9oz lean minced lamb
1 garlic clove, crushed
1 tsp each ground cumin
and coriander
2 tbsp natural yogurt
2 tbsp pine nuts
a handful of fresh mint, chopped
(or use a sprinkling of dried mint)

Takes 25 minutes • Serves 4

1 Preheat the oven to 220°C/fan 200°C/ Gas 7. Make the bread mix following the packet instructions, then divide the dough into two and roll out into large ovals. Transfer to a large, floured baking sheet.
2 In a bowl, combine the onion, lamb, garlic, spices and yogurt, then season. Crumble the mixture over the dough almost to the edges, then scatter over the pine nuts. Bake for 15–18 minutes until the bread is golden and crisp and the meat is browned. Sprinkle over the mint before serving.

• Per serving 377 kcalories, protein 22g, carbohydrate 47g, fat 12g, saturated fat 4g, fibre 3g, sugar 3g, salt 1.24g

You've probably got most of the ingredients for this hearty soup in your kitchen already. This recipe has a low GI and is low in saturated fat, but if you wish you can serve with home- or ready-made croûtons.

Winter minestrone

2 tbsp olive oil
1 onion, chopped
100g/4oz chopped streaky bacon
2 large carrots, chopped
2 sticks celery, chopped
1 medium potato, peeled and chopped
2 garlic cloves, finely chopped or crushed
400g can chopped tomatoes
1 litre/1¾ pints vegetable stock
2 tsp chopped sage leaves, or 1 tsp dried
a few cabbage leaves, shredded (or use any other greens)
400g can haricot beans
a handful of chopped parsley
croûtons or crusty bread, to serve (optional)

Takes 55 minutes • Serves 4

1 Heat the olive oil in a large pan, add the onion and bacon, and fry for about 5 minutes until the onion is starting to brown. Tip in the carrots, celery, potato and garlic, stir well and cook for a few minutes.
2 Add the tomatoes, stock and sage, then bring to the boil, stirring. Reduce the heat to a simmer and cook, partly covered, for 30 minutes, stirring in the cabbage after 15 minutes. Drain and rinse the beans, and add to the pan with the parsley. Season and serve with croûtons or crusty bread, if you like.

• Per serving 274 kcalories, protein 13g, carbohydrate 28g, fat 13g, saturated fat 3g, fibre 8g, sugar 12g, salt 2.56g

Summery stuffed peppers with a taste of Mexico make a great midweek supper that's also low in fat. Pick flat-bottomed peppers so they stand up as they bake.

Salsa chicken peppers

140g/5oz Camargue red rice (or use brown rice)
4 large red peppers
oil, for brushing
270g jar hot salsa (we used Discovery)
200g/8oz cooked chicken, chopped
200g can red kidney beans, drained
40g/1½oz mature Cheddar, grated
20g pack coriander, leaves chopped
lime wedges, to squeeze
avocado salad, to serve (optional)

Takes 40 minutes • Serves 4

1 Boil the rice for 25 minutes until just tender. Meanwhile, preheat the oven to 220°C/fan 200°C/Gas 7.
2 Slice the tops off the peppers and scoop out the seeds. Lightly oil the peppers and their lids and bake in a roasting tin for 12 minutes.
3 Drain the rice and mix with the salsa, chicken, beans, Cheddar and coriander. Season to taste. Take the peppers out of the oven, then fill them with the rice mixture. Put on the lids, return them to the oven and bake for 10 minutes. Squeeze over lime wedges and serve with an avocado salad.

• Per serving 370 kcalories, protein 24g, carbohydrate 50g, fat 10g, saturated fat 4g, fibre 5g, sugar 15g, salt 1.65g

Curry spices and fresh coriander turn these low-fat turkey burgers into something tasty and special.

Spiced turkey burgers

500g/1lb 2oz turkey mince
½ red onion, grated
1 garlic clove, crushed
2 tsp Madras curry powder
a handful of chopped fresh coriander
1 egg yolk
1 tbsp sunflower oil
4 burger buns
salad and mango chutney or lime pickle, to serve

Takes 20 minutes • Serves 4

1 In a large bowl, mix together the turkey mince, onion, garlic, curry powder, coriander and egg yolk with a little salt and pepper. Combine well with your hands, then shape into four flat burger patties.
2 Heat the oil in a frying pan over a high heat then cook the burgers for 5 minutes each or until cooked through. Slice the burger buns in half and toast the cut sides. Place the salad on the bottom halves of the warm buns, then top with the burgers and chutney or lime pickle.

• Per serving 318 kcalories, protein 34g, carbohydrate 26g, fat 9g, saturated fat 2g, fibre 2g, sugar 2g, salt 0.95g

Meaty tuna goes fabulously with ginger, garlic and soy. This superhealthy dish is the ideal supper for hungry schoolchildren, being a good source of omega 3 as well as low in saturated fat and salt.

Tangy tuna burgers

200g/8oz fresh tuna steaks
1 garlic clove, finely chopped
a small knob of fresh root ginger, peeled and finely chopped
1 tbsp soy sauce
a handful of coriander leaves, chopped
1 tbsp sunflower oil
burger buns and lettuce leaves, tomatoes and avocado, all sliced, to serve

Takes 25 minutes • Serves 2

1 Chop the tuna into small chunks, then carry on chopping until it is roughly minced. Tip the tuna into a bowl and mix with the garlic, ginger, soy sauce and coriander. Shape into two burgers, place on a plate, then put in the freezer for 10 minutes to firm up.

2 Heat the oil in a non-stick frying pan, then cook the burgers for 1–2 minutes on each side or until done to your liking. Slice the burger buns in half and toast. Serve the burgers in toasted buns with some lettuce, tomato and avocado.

• Per burger (without bun) 97 kcalories, protein 12g, carbohydrate 1g, fat 5g, saturated fat 1g, fibre none, sugar none, salt 0.74g

There's something very comforting about garlic mushrooms – here they compliment flaky, white fish perfectly to create a luxurious low-fat meal. Serve with green vegetables.

Crumbed fish with garlic mushrooms

1 tbsp olive oil
3 garlic cloves, crushed
250g pack chestnut mushrooms, thickly sliced
1 small bunch parsley, leaves roughly chopped
4 × 140g/5oz fish fillets, such as cod or haddock
1 thick slice white or brown bread, torn into small pieces
50g/2oz Cheddar, grated

Takes 20 minutes • Serves 4

1 Heat the oil in an ovenproof frying pan, then fry the garlic and mushrooms for 5 minutes until softened but not coloured. Throw in the parsley and mix together.
2 Push the mixture to one side, place the fish in the pan, season, then spoon the mixture over the fish.
3 Heat the grill to High. Remove the fish from the heat, sprinkle over the bread and cheese, then grill for 5 minutes or until the fish flakes easily.

• Per serving 227 kcalories, protein 31g, carbohydrate 7g, fat 9g, saturated fat 3g, fibre 1g, sugar 1g, salt 0.6g

You'll find this the simplest of sauces. It's low in saturated fat and salt, and works really well with chicken and prawns too.

Tomato and thyme fish

1 tbsp olive oil
1 onion, chopped
400g can chopped tomatoes
1 heaped tsp light brown soft sugar
a few fresh thyme sprigs, leaves stripped
1 tbsp soy sauce
4 fillets sustainable white fish

Takes 20 minutes • Serves 4

1 Heat the oil in a frying pan, add the onion, then fry for 5–8 minutes until lightly browned. Stir in the tomatoes, sugar, thyme and soy sauce, then bring to the boil.
2 Simmer for 5 minutes, then carefully slip the fish into the sauce. Cover and gently cook for 8–10 minutes until the cod flakes easily. Serve with baked or steamed potatoes.

• Per serving 172 kcalories, protein 27g, carbohydrate 7g, fat 4g, saturated fat 1g, fibre 1g, sugar 6g, salt 1.1g

This recipe suits any greens you have to hand – from shredded kale to Brussels sprouts – and goes well with chicken or fish. It's a good source of vitamin C and folic acid, and gives you two of your 5-a-day.

Indian-spiced greens

1 tbsp vegetable oil
1 tsp cumin seeds
½ tsp black mustard seeds
4 green chillies, seeded and finely chopped
large piece fresh root ginger, grated
½ tsp turmeric
500g/1lb 2oz shredded greens
100g/4oz frozen peas
juice of 1 lemon
½ tsp ground coriander
1 small bunch coriander, roughly chopped
2 tbsp unsweetened desiccated coconut

Takes 20 minutes • Serves 4

1 Heat the oil in a large non-stick pan or wok, sizzle the cumin and mustard seeds for 1 minute, then add the chillies, ginger and turmeric. Fry until aromatic, then add the greens, a pinch of salt, a splash of water and the peas. Cover the pan and cook for 4–5 minutes until the greens have wilted.
2 Add the lemon juice, ground coriander, half the fresh coriander and half the desiccated coconut, then toss everything together. Pile into a serving dish and scatter with the rest of the coconut and coriander.

• Per serving 117 kcalories, protein 5g, carbohydrate 9g, fat 7g, saturated fat 3g, fibre 5g, sugar 6g, salt 0.03g

A cross between French classic potato dishes, dauphinoise and boulangère, this low-fat bake makes a handsome accompaniment for any roast and is a good source of vitamin C.

Leek, potato and bacon bake

600ml/1 pint vegetable or chicken stock
1kg/2lb 4oz floury potatoes, thinly sliced
6 leeks, trimmed and washed thinly sliced into rounds
25g/1oz butter
3–4 rashers rindless streaky bacon, chopped
3 tbsp double cream (optional)

Takes 1 hour • Serves 8

1 Preheat the oven to 200°C/fan 180°C/ Gas 6. Put the stock in a large pan, bring to the boil, then add the potatoes and the leeks. Bring back to the boil for 5 minutes, then drain well, reserving the stock in a jug.
2 Meanwhile, lightly butter a large baking dish. Layer up the potatoes and leeks higgledy-piggledy, seasoning as you go, then scatter the bacon over the top. Season well, pour over 150ml/¼ pint of the reserved stock, then spoon over the cream (if using) and cover with foil. Bake for 40 minutes, uncovering it halfway through so that the bacon crisps.

• Per serving (without cream) 153 kcalories, protein 5g, carbohydrate 24g, fat 5g, saturated fat 2g, fibre 4g, sugar 3g, salt 0.35g

Roasting brings out the best in lots of vegetables, but peppers top the list. This is a perfect low-fat, low-salt side to roast chicken or fish.

Cumin roast peppers, tomatoes and olives

4 red peppers, seeded and cut into chunky pieces
3 tbsp olive oil
2 × 300g packs cherry tomatoes on the vine (or use smallish tomatoes and halve them)
1 tsp cumin seed
100g/4oz fat green olives

Takes 40 minutes • Serves 6

1 Preheat the oven to 200°C/fan 180°C/ Gas 6. Put the peppers in a medium-sized roasting tin (or an ovenproof frying pan will do) and splash with two tablespoons of the oil. Season generously, then roast for about 20 minutes or until softened a little.
2 Remove the tin from the oven, sit the bunches of tomatoes among the peppers, scatter the cumin over everything, then drizzle with the rest of the oil. Season again, then return to the oven and roast for about 10 minutes or until the tomato skins have split. Toss the olives through just before serving either warm or cold.

• Per serving 116 kcalories, protein 2g, carbohydrate 10g, fat 8g, saturated fat 1g, fibre 3g, sugar 9g, salt 0.81g

A tasty accompaniment for a summery lunch or supper that's high in fibre and vitamin C, and provides four of your 5-a-day.

Ratatouille

2 red or yellow peppers
4 large ripe tomatoes
5 tbsp olive oil
2 large aubergines, cut into large chunks
4 small courgettes, thickly sliced
1 medium onion, thinly sliced
3 garlic cloves, crushed
1 tbsp red wine vinegar
1 tsp sugar
a small bunch of basil, leaves torn

Takes 45 minutes • Serves 4

1 Peel the peppers using a potato peeler, then remove the seeds and cut into large chunks. Score a small cross on the base of each tomato, then cover with boiling water. Leave for 20 seconds, then cool in a bowl of cold water. Peel, deseed and roughly chop the flesh.

2 Heat two tablespoons of oil in a large frying pan then brown the aubergines for 5 minutes all over, until soft. Set aside then fry the courgettes in another tablespoon of oil for 5 minutes or until golden. Fry the peppers and onion, then add the garlic and fry for a further minute.

3 Stir in the vinegar and sugar, then tip in the tomatoes and half the basil. Return the rest of the vegetables to the pan with some salt and pepper and cook for 5 minutes. Serve with the remaining basil scattered over.

• Per serving 241 kcalories, protein 6g, carbohydrate 20g, fat 16g, saturated fat 2g, fibre 8g, sugar 18g, salt 0.05g

This makes a great side dish for any roast or casserole. It tastes even better if you make it earlier in the day and reheat it for serving. It's low in both saturated fat and salt, and gives you two of your 5-a-day.

Gratin of winter vegetables

500g/1lb 2oz carrots
1 medium celeriac
1kg/2lb 4oz floury potatoes, such as King Edward
5 tbsp olive oil
1 garlic clove, finely chopped
300ml/½ pint hot vegetable stock
a handful of chopped parsley, to serve

Takes 1¼ hours • Serves 8

1 Preheat the oven to 190°C/fan 170°C/ Gas 5. Peel the carrots, celeriac and potatoes and slice thinly by hand or with the slicing blade of the food processor, keeping the cut vegetables separate.

2 Arrange half the potatoes in a gratin dish and drizzle with one tablespoon of the oil and a little garlic. Cover with the celeriac, more oil and garlic, then the carrot and more oil and garlic. Season each layer. Cover with the remaining potatoes and drizzle with oil.

3 Pour over the stock, then cover the dish tightly with foil. Bake for 45 minutes, then remove the foil and cook for a further 35–45 minutes or until the vegetables are tender and the top is golden and crisp. If you're making in advance, reheat in the oven for 15–20 minutes. Scatter with parsley before serving.

• Per serving 173 kcalories, protein 4g, carbohydrate 23g, fat 8g, saturated fat 1g, fibre 5g, sugar 6g, salt 0.41g

A sophisticated salad that's easily doubled if you're entertaining. Serve this superhealthy dish when the sun shines – it's packed with vitamin C and folic acid, high in fibre and counts as four of your 5-a-day.

Chicken and orange salad

150g pack green beans, trimmed
1 large avocado
100g bag watercress, roughly chopped
1 fennel bulb, finely sliced
2 oranges
2 tbsp olive oil
2 cooked boneless, skinless chicken breasts, shredded

Takes 15 minutes • Serves 2

1 Cook the beans in a large pan of boiling salted water for 4–5 minutes. Drain and cool under cold water, then put in a serving bowl.
2 Peel and slice the avocado and add to the bowl with the watercress and fennel. Peel the oranges, then cut out the segments and add them to the bowl. Squeeze the rest of the orange juice into a small bowl and mix with the olive oil to make a dressing. Toss the salad in the dressing, scatter over the chicken, then serve.

• Per serving 572 kcalories, protein 45g, carbohydrate 19g, fat 36g, saturated fat 5g, fibre 10g, sugar 17g, salt 0.30g

Try this for a light, low-fat supper, or add some cooked egg noodles to make a more substantial salad.

Spicy chicken salad with broccoli

2 broccoli heads, cut into florets
2 tbsp olive oil
5 shallots or 1 large onion, finely sliced
2 red chillies, seeded and sliced
2 garlic cloves, sliced
a handful of pitted black olives
4 roast chicken breasts, sliced
4 tbsp soy sauce

Takes 25 minutes • Serves 4

1 Steam the broccoli for 4 minutes until just tender, tip into a large bowl, then season. Meanwhile, heat the oil in a pan and fry the shallots or onion for 2 minutes. Add the chillies and garlic, then cook for a further 4 minutes until softened. Lift out the shallots, chillies and garlic with a slotted spoon, then mix with the broccoli, olives and chicken in a bowl.
2 Add the soy sauce to the pan, warm it over a medium heat, then pour it over the salad. Eat warm or cold.

• Per serving 291 kcalories, protein 42g, carbohydrate 4g, fat 12g, saturated fat 2g, fibre 3g, sugar 3g, salt 3.05g

This high-fibre dish provides all five of your 5-a-day and makes a great lunch dish or accompaniment to pasta. You'll find the veg absorb the most flavour from the dressing when dressed slightly warm.

Warm pesto roast veg

3 parsnips, peeled and sliced
2 red onions, sliced
2 red peppers, seeded and sliced
1 small butternut squash, peeled and sliced
2 tbsp olive or sunflower oil
1 garlic clove, crushed
4 tbsp basil pesto (tubs from the chiller cabinet have the best flavour)
100g/4oz baby spinach leaves
2 tbsp pine nuts, toasted

Takes 45 minutes • Serves 4

1 Preheat the oven to 230°C/fan 210°C/ Gas 8. Put all the vegetables in a roasting tin with the oil, garlic, and a seasoning of salt and black pepper, then rub with your hands until evenly coated. Roast for 30 minutes until golden and soft.

2 Allow to cool slightly, then tip into a large bowl. Mix with the basil pesto, spinach leaves and toasted pine nuts, then serve.

• Per serving 306 kcalories, protein 10g, carbohydrate 35g, fat 15g, saturated fat 3g, fibre 10g, sugar 20g, salt 0.32g

Cool yet fiery, this Asian-inspired cucumber salad is a barbecue must. It's great served with chicken and, as a fresh-tasting, low-fat dish, it also cuts through the richness of grilled steak.

Spicy cucumber salad

1 large cucumber, peeled
1 tsp golden caster sugar
1 tbsp rice or white wine vinegar
2 tbsp soy sauce
1 tbsp sesame oil
a small knob of fresh root ginger, finely chopped
2 garlic cloves, finely chopped
1 large red chilli, halved, seeded and finely sliced
2 spring onions, finely sliced
a large handful of coriander leaves
Grilled chicken, to serve (optional)

Takes 35 minutes • Serves 4

1 Slice the cucumber in half lengthways, use a teaspoon to scoop out the seeds, then discard. Slice it into thick diagonal chunks, tip them into a bowl and sprinkle with the sugar, vinegar and large pinch of salt. Leave for about 30 minutes in the fridge.

2 Meanwhile, tip the remaining ingredients into a bowl. Drain the cucumber from its marinade and tip it in with the rest of the ingredients. Serve with grilled chicken or your choice of meat or fish.

• Per serving 238 kcalories, protein 33g, carbohydrate 5g, fat 9g, saturated fat 2g, fibre 1g, sugar 4g, salt 2.17g

Serve these aubergines as a starter, an accompaniment to meat or as a sandwich filling. This dish is low in saturated fat and salt.

Griddled aubergines with yogurt and mint

4 small aubergines, sliced into 1cm/½in thick rounds
2 tbsp olive oil
150g pot natural yogurt
juice of ½ lemon
2 garlic cloves, crushed
1 small bunch mint leaves, coarsely chopped

Takes 45 minutes • Serves 4

1 Drizzle the aubergine slices with olive oil and a little salt and pepper, and toss in a bowl. Heat a griddle pan until hot and cook the slices on both sides until soft and lightly charred; you'll need to do this in batches. Leave to cool slightly on a serving plate.
2 Meanwhile, mix the yogurt with the lemon juice, garlic and mint in a bowl. Season the mixture to taste. Drizzle the yogurt mixture over the griddled aubergine and serve at room temperature.

• Per serving 105 kcalories, protein 4g, carbohydrate 8g, fat 7g, saturated fat 1g, fibre 4g, sugar 6g, salt 0.33g

There's masses of crunch, flavour and colour in this versatile Asian side dish. It is also a superhealthy source of vitamin C and folic acid as well as being low in saturated fat and salt.

Broccoli with cashews and oyster sauce

1 tbsp sunflower oil
100g/4oz unsalted cashews
2 heads broccoli, cut into smallish florets
3 tbsp oyster sauce, or more to taste

Takes 25 minutes • Serves 6

1 Heat a little of the oil in a wok and toast the cashew nuts until they start to turn golden. Tip out of the pan, then add the rest of the oil. Stir fry the broccoli for 2–3 minutes until it has turned bright green (it will still be very firm).

2 Add a splash of water to the pan, then cover with a lid and steam for about 4 minutes or until the stems just give with a knife. Push to the side of the pan, then pour the oyster sauce into the other side. Bring to the boil, then stir into the broccoli. Toss in the cashews and serve with simply cooked fish or chicken and some boiled rice or noodles.

• Per serving 156 kcalories, protein 8g, carbohydrate 6g, fat 11g, saturated fat 1g, fibre 4g, sugar 4g, salt 0.82g

As there are no leaves to go droopy in this salad, it's a great one to transport – the perfect low-fat contribution to a picnic or bring-a-dish dinner party.

Stir-fry noodle salad

4 blocks egg noodles
4 tbsp sesame oil
2 red peppers, seeded and finely sliced
2 carrots, sliced into batons
a large knob of fresh root ginger, finely chopped
2 garlic cloves, finely chopped
4 kaffir lime leaves (from supermarkets and oriental food stores)
1 bunch spring onions, finely sliced
6 tbsp soy sauce
2 large handfuls of beansprouts
250g block tofu, cut into cubes
1 large bunch coriander, stalks finely chopped, leaves roughly chopped

FOR THE DRESSING
150ml/¼ pint rice wine vinegar
2 sticks of lemongrass
a small piece of fresh red chilli (about ⅓ of a chilli)
2 tbsp golden caster sugar
4 kaffir lime leaves, torn

Takes 25 minutes • Serves 6

1 First, make the dressing. Tip all the ingredients into a small pan and bring to a simmer. Boil for 1 minute, then remove from the heat to infuse.
2 Cook the noodles according to the packet instructions, then drain and toss with three tablespoons of the sesame oil. Leave to cool, tossing occasionally to prevent them sticking.
3 Heat the rest of the oil in a wok and stir fry the peppers, carrots, ginger and garlic for just 1 minute, then set aside.
4 To serve, tip the noodles into a bowl and pour over the dressing. Finely shred the lime leaves and toss in with all the other ingredients, setting aside a small handful of coriander leaves. Taste, adding a splash more vinegar, soy or sesame oil, if you like. Scatter over the rest of the coriander and serve.

• Per serving 301 kcalories, protein 10g, carbohydrate 44g, fat 11g, saturated fat 1g, fibre 3g, sugar 14g, salt 3.35g

The fresh colours and flavours of this salad are so summery. The salad ingredients here will give you one of your 5-a-day.

Prawn and avocado platter with lime and chilli

350g/12oz large headless cooked prawns, unpeeled
2 avocados
a large handful of basil leaves
120g bag baby leaf salad
lime wedges, to serve

FOR THE DRESSING
2 tbsp fresh lime juice
2 tsp clear honey
1 red chilli, seeded and finely chopped
3 tbsp light olive oil

Takes 25 minutes • Serves 4

1 Peel the prawns, leaving the tails intact, then rinse and pat dry. Put all the dressing ingredients into a small bowl and whisk to mix.
2 Up to 1 hour before serving, peel and stone the avocados, then cut them into thick slices and put them in a large bowl with half the dressing. Mix lightly to coat all the slices (this prevents them turning brown).
3 Chop the basil and add to the bowl along with the prawns. Toss everything together lightly.
4 Scatter the baby salad leaves over a platter, then spoon over the prawns, avocado and basil mix. Drizzle with the set-aside dressing and serve with lime wedges for squeezing over.

• Per serving 266 kcalories, protein 15g, carbohydrate 4g, fat 21g, saturated fat 3g, fibre 2g, sugar 12g, salt 1.08g

Try serving this low-fat, low-salt salad with a summery roast chicken or leg of lamb, or as part of a barbecue menu.

Couscous and chickpea salad

250g/9oz couscous
1 tbsp harissa (we recommend Belazu Rose Harissa)
50g/2oz raisins
6 soft dried apricots, chopped
400g can chickpeas, drained and rinsed
3 tbsp pine nuts, lightly toasted
juice of 1 lemon
4 tbsp olive oil

Takes 25 minutes • Serves 6

1 Make up the couscous according to the packet instructions, adding the harissa, raisins and apricots with the recommended amount of water. Toss in the remaining ingredients then cover for 10 minutes or until all of the liquid has been absorbed. Fluff up with a fork and serve – or keep it covered until needed.

• Per serving 289 kcalories, protein 7g, carbohydrate 38g, fat 13g, saturated fat 2g, fibre 3g, sugar 10g, salt 0.29g

Ring the changes to your usual potato salad – this one goes well with salmon or smoked mackerel fillets. Low in saturated fat and salt, this salad is a good source of folic acid and provides one of your 5-a-day.

Beetroot and potato salad

500g pack new potatoes
4 tbsp olive oil
1 tbsp white wine vinegar
2 garlic cloves, chopped
1 red onion, finely chopped
2 × 250g packs cooked beetroot, diced
20g pack coriander leaves, chopped

Takes 35 minutes • Serves 6

1 Boil the potatoes in salted water until tender, about 15 minutes, then chop them when cool enough to handle. You can take off the skins or leave them on – the choice is yours.
2 Meanwhile, mix the oil, vinegar, garlic and onion with the beetroot. Toss in the potatoes and coriander. This can be made a day ahead, but, if you do, add the coriander just before serving.

• Per serving 171 kcalories, protein 4g, carbohydrate 23g, fat 8g, saturated fat 1g, fibre 3g, sugar 9g, salt 0.26g

This zingy salad provides three of your 5-a-day and is low in saturated fat and salt.

No-cook Asian prawn coleslaw

½ head white cabbage, finely shredded
1 large carrot, coarsely grated
100g/4oz radishes, sliced
2 large handfuls of beansprouts
a handful of cashew nuts
a handful of fresh coriander leaves
100g/4oz cooked prawns

FOR THE DRESSING
zest and juice of 1 lime
2 tsp sugar
1 tbsp sesame oil
1 red chilli, seeded and chopped (optional)
a small knob of fresh root ginger, finely shredded

Takes 15 minutes • Serves 2

1 Mix all the dressing ingredients together in a large bowl, including the chilli, if using.
2 Stir all the other ingredients, except the prawns, into the dressing. Pile the salad on to two plates, then top with a handful of prawns.

• Per serving 334 kcalories, protein 19.9g, carbohydrate 28.2g, fat 16.6g, saturated fat 2g, fibre 7.9g, sugar 24.2g, salt 1g

Sweet, just-cooked peas counter the punch of the horseradish dressing beautifully in this easy, low-fat salad.

Ham and beetroot salad bowl

100g/4oz frozen peas
175g/6oz cooked beetroot
2 spring onions, thinly sliced
2 tbsp Greek yogurt
2 tsp horseradish sauce
½ iceberg lettuce, shredded
100g/4oz wafer-thin ham, sliced

Takes 15 minutes • Serves 2

1 Pour boiling water over the peas and leave for 2 minutes, then drain well. Cut the beetroot into cubes.

2 Tip the peas, beetroot and spring onions into a bowl and mix well. Mix the yogurt and horseradish together in a small bowl, then add about one tablespoon of boiling water to make a pouring sauce.

3 Pile the lettuce into bowls and spoon over the beetroot mix. Thinly drizzle the dressing over the salad and top with the sliced ham.

• Per serving 166 kcalories, protein 16g, carbohydrate 17g, fat 4g, saturated fat 2g, fibre 5g, sugar 13g, salt 1.92g

Five storecupboard ingredients cleverly come together in this light, low-fat lemony risotto. Substitute the peas for some asparagus when it's in season.

Lemon and pea risotto

200g/8oz risotto rice
850ml/1½ pints hot vegetable stock
50g/2oz frozen garden peas or petits pois
50g/2oz Parmesan, grated, plus extra to serve
juice and zest of ½ lemon

Takes 30 minutes • Serves 2

1 Heat a large pan over a medium heat, then toast the rice, stirring constantly, for 1 minute. Add one ladleful of the hot stock and stir until absorbed. Reduce the heat. Add the rest of the stock, a ladleful at a time, until the rice is almost cooked and stock is absorbed – about 20 minutes.
2 Stir in the peas, cooking for 3–5 minutes, then remove the pan from the heat. Add the cheese, lemon juice and seasoning, then stir. Scatter with the lemon zest, then serve immediately with extra grated Parmesan.

• Per serving 477 kcalories, protein 20g, carbohydrate 84g, fat 9g, saturated fat 5g, fibre 5g, sugar 4g, salt 1.04g

Warm up with a bowl of superhealthy, spicy lentils – low in fat, high in fibre, a good source of iron and four of your 5-a-day. Parsnip crisps made this way are a healthy alternative to shop-bought versions.

Red lentil dhal with crisp parsnips

1 tbsp sunflower oil, plus 1 tsp
2 onions, chopped
200g/8oz red split lentils, rinsed
1–2 tbsp curry powder
400g can chopped tomatoes
850ml/1½ pints hot vegetable stock
2 parsnips

Takes 20 minutes • Serves 4

1 Preheat the oven to 200°C/fan 180°C/ Gas 6. Heat the oil in a pan, add the onions, then fry until lightly coloured, about 2 minutes. Stir in lentils and curry powder, then add the tomatoes and stock. Bring to the boil. Reduce the heat, cover, then simmer for 10–12 minutes, until the lentils are tender.
2 Peel the parsnips and shave them into strips. Toss them in one teaspoon of oil in a roasting tin and bake in the oven for 10 minutes or until crisp. Spoon the lentil dhal into four bowls and pile the parsnip crisps on top.

• Per serving 295 kcalories, protein 16g, carbohydrate 48g, fat 6g, saturated fat 1g, fibre 9g, sugar 13g, salt 0.5g

Thai curry paste adds a taste of the exotic to everyday vegetables in this quick and easy one-pot. A good source of vitamin C, this low-fat curry provides two of your 5-a-day.

Thai-spiced veggie curry

1 tbsp sunflower oil
1 butternut squash, peeled and cut into thick slices
1 onion, sliced
1 tbsp Thai red curry paste
50g sachet coconut cream
250g/9oz frozen French beans
naan bread, to serve (optional)

Takes 35 minutes • Serves 4

1 Heat the oil in a pan. Tip in the squash and onion, then gently fry for about 5 minutes until soft, but not brown. Tip in the curry paste and cook for 1 minute more. Stir the coconut cream together with 300ml/½ pint boiling water, then pour it into the pan. Bring to the boil and simmer for 10 minutes.
2 Add the beans to the pan, then cook for about 3–5 minutes more until everything is just tender. Serve with warmed naan bread.

• Per serving 178 kcalories, protein 5g, carbohydrate 23g, fat 9g, saturated fat 4g, fibre 5g, sugar 13g, salt 0.17g

Chestnut mushrooms add masses of flavour to this family-friendly, low-fat pasta dish, which will also provide you with one of your 5-a-day.

Rigatoni with rich mushroom sauce

½ × 40g pack dried mushrooms
300g/10oz rigatoni
2 tsp olive oil
1 red onion, finely chopped
300g/10oz chestnut mushrooms, sliced
a few fresh thyme sprigs or good pinch dried thyme
2 tsp tomato purée

Takes 25 minutes • Serves 4

1 Soak the dried mushrooms in 175ml/ 6fl oz boiling water. Cook the pasta in a large pan of boiling water, according to the packet instructions.
2 Meanwhile, heat the oil in a pan, add the onion and fry gently for 5 minutes until softened. Drain the soaked mushrooms and finely chop. Stir the fresh and soaked mushrooms, thyme and tomato purée into the onion, then add 150ml/¼ pint of the mushroom-soaking liquid, discarding the last 50ml/2fl oz left in the bowl. Bring to the boil.
3 Reduce the heat and simmer for 5 minutes until the mushrooms are tender. Drain the pasta, return to the pan and combine with the mushroom sauce.

• Per serving 304 kcalories, protein 11.9g, carbohydrate 59.8g, fat 3.6g, saturated fat 0.5g, fibre 4.2g, sugar 3.7g, salt 0.06g

Get all of your 5-a-day in one meal with this vibrant suppertime dish. This low-fat, high-fibre pasta makes a fantastic lunchbox filler too.

Roasted ratatouille pasta

1 small aubergine, trimmed and cut into chunks
1 red pepper, halved, seeded and cut into chunks
1 courgette, trimmed and cut into chunks
1 red onion, thinly sliced
2 garlic cloves, unpeeled and left whole
1 tbsp olive oil
200g/8oz ripe tomatoes, chopped
175g/6oz penne
a good handful of basil leaves

Takes 45 minutes • Serves 2

1 Preheat the oven to 200°C/fan 180°C/Gas 6. Tip all the fresh vegetables into a roasting tin, drizzle over the oil, then season and toss together. Roast for 20 minutes, add the tomatoes, then roast for a further 10 minutes.
2 Cook the pasta, drain and reserve four tablespoons of water. Tip the pasta, the water and the basil leaves into the vegetables and toss together. Squeeze over the soft garlic before serving.

• Per serving 450 kcalories, protein 15g, carbohydrate 83g, fat 9g, saturated fat 1g, fibre 9g, sugar 16g, salt 0.07g

Keep a box of eggs in the fridge and you're never far from a good meal. They're a healthy option, too, and combined with all these veggies, this dish gives you three of your 5-a-day.

Egg curry

3 eggs
1 onion, finely sliced
1 tbsp vegetable oil
2 tbsp korma curry paste
175g/6oz green beans, trimmed and halved
175g/6oz young spinach leaves
175g/6oz cherry tomatoes
100ml/3½fl oz reduced-fat coconut milk
naan or pitta breads, to serve (optional)

Takes 30 minutes • Serves 2

1 Put the eggs into a pan of cold water, bring to the boil, then cook for 8 minutes. Drain and cool them under cold, running water, then peel off the shells. Fry the onion in the oil for about 5 minutes, until softened and lightly coloured, then stir in the curry paste and beans.

2 Add 200ml/8fl oz water, then cover and cook for 5 minutes. Add the spinach, tomatoes and coconut milk, then bring to a simmer, stirring until the spinach is just wilted. Spoon on to two plates, then halve the eggs and sit them on top. Serve with toasted naan or pitta breads.

• Per serving 351 kcalories, protein 18g, carbohydrate 14g, fat 26g, saturated fat 8g, fibre 6g, sugar 10g, salt 1.38g

Topped with melting, garlicky Gruyère, these big, juicy low-fat burgers
will appeal to everyone – veggie or not.

Portabello burgers

4 portabello or field mushrooms,
stalks trimmed
1 tsp sunflower oil
50g/2oz Gruyère, grated
1 garlic clove, crushed
1 tbsp butter, softened
4 ciabatta or burger buns, split
and toasted
lettuce, tomatoes and sliced red
onion, to serve

Takes 20 minutes • Serves 4

1 Heat the grill to High. Rub the mushrooms
with oil and set on a baking sheet. Grill for
3 minutes on each side until cooked, but
still firm.
2 Mix the cheese, garlic, butter and
seasoning in a bowl, then spoon into the
mushrooms. Grill until the cheese melts, then
stuff into the toasted buns with the salad.

• Per serving 228 kcalories, protein 11g, carbohydrate
23g, fat 11g, saturated fat 5g, fibre 3g, sugar 1g,
salt 1.05g

Bought pizzas never taste this good – nor do you as much good. This dish is low in saturated fat and salt, a good source of calcium and vitamin C, and also provides two of your 5-a-day.

Frying-pan pizza

1 yellow pepper, seeded and cut into chunks
1 courgette, thickly sliced
1 red onion, cut into wedges
2 tbsp olive oil, plus 1 tsp for drizzling
225g/8oz self-raising flour
5 tbsp fresh tomato pasta sauce
50g/2oz strong Cheddar, grated

Takes 45 minutes • Serves 4

1 Preheat the oven to 220°C/fan 200°C/Gas 7. Place the pepper, courgette and onion on a baking sheet and drizzle with a teaspoon of olive oil. Roast in the oven for 20 minutes or until soft and beginning to brown. Set aside.
2 Heat the grill to Medium. Season the flour well and mix with the remaining oil and 4–5 tablespoons of water to form a soft dough. Knead briefly, then roll out on a floured surface to a rough 20cm/8in circle.
3 Transfer the dough to an ovenproof, non-stick frying pan and fry over a medium heat for 5 minutes or until the underside begins to brown. Turn over and fry for 5 minutes.
4 Spread the tomato sauce over the base, scatter with the veg, then sprinkle with cheese. Grill the pizza for 3–4 minutes until the cheese has melted. Slice into wedges.

• Per serving 331 kcalories, protein 10g, carbohydrate 49g, fat 12g, saturated fat 4g, fibre 3g, sugar 6g, salt 0.89g

Sesame oil is the key to this recipe, giving nutty depth to the whole dish and keeping it low in saturated fat.

Sesame noodles with tofu

250g pack firm tofu, drained
2 tbsp reduced-salt soy sauce, plus extra to serve (optional)
1 tbsp sesame oil, plus extra to serve (optional)
300g/10oz green vegetables (we used mangetout and halved bok choi)
1 garlic clove, sliced
a small knob of fresh root ginger, peeled and shredded
300g pack straight-to-wok egg noodles (or use 2 sheets of medium dried egg noodles and follow packet instructions)
1 tbsp sesame seeds

Takes 10 minutes • Serves 2

1 Cut the tofu into 12 pieces and mix with one tablespoon of soy sauce and 1 teaspoon of the sesame oil. Heat the remaining oil in a wok, then stir fry the vegetables, garlic and ginger for 2 minutes until the vegetables are starting to wilt. Drizzle with two tablespoons of water, then stir fry for another minute.

2 Add the noodles, sesame seeds and soy sauce from the marinated tofu, then stir fry for 2 minutes. Now add the tofu, splash over the remaining one tablespoon of soy sauce, then cover with a lid or baking sheet. Leave on the heat for 1 minute so that the tofu heats through, then gently mix the stir fry to combine.

3 Divide between two bowls and splash over a little more soy sauce and sesame oil to serve, if you like.

• Per serving 531 kcalories, protein 27g, carbohydrate 74g, fat 17g, saturated fat 2g, fibre 5g, sugar 6g, salt 3.35g

A large omelette makes a great family supper. This one is ideal for all ages, as it's a good source of folic acid and low in saturated fat and salt.

Spanish spinach omelette

400g bag spinach leaves
3 tbsp olive oil
1 large onion, finely sliced
2 large peeled and cooked potatoes, thickly sliced
10 eggs

Takes 30 minutes • Cuts into 8 wedges

1 Tip the spinach into a large colander and bring a kettleful of water to the boil. Slowly pour the boiling water over the spinach until wilted, then cool the leaves under cold water. Squeeze all the liquid out of the spinach and set aside.

2 Heat the oil in a non-stick frying pan and gently cook the onion for 10 minutes until soft.

3 Heat the grill to High. While the onion is cooking, beat the eggs together in a large bowl and season with salt and pepper. Stir the spinach and the potatoes into the pan, then pour in the eggs. Cook, stirring occasionally until nearly set, then grill for a few minutes until just set all the way through. Flip on to a board and cut into wedges.

• Per wedge 209 kcalories, protein 12g, carbohydrate 11g, fat 13g, saturated fat 3g, fibre 2g, sugar 2g, salt 0.46g

A little cheese can go a long way in this low-fat, yet filling, simple dish. Perfect served with a crisp, green salad.

Roasted squash and goat's cheese gnocchi

450g/1lb butternut squash, peeled , seeded and cut into small chunks
1 garlic clove
2 tbsp olive oil
500g pack fresh potato gnocchi
200g/8oz young spinach leaves
100g/4oz soft goat's cheese

Takes 35 minutes • Serves 4

1 Preheat the oven to 200°C/fan 180°C/ Gas 6. Tip the squash into a roasting tin with the garlic and oil, and some salt and pepper and mix well. Roast for 20 minutes, shaking the pan halfway through, until tender and golden.

2 Meanwhile, boil the gnocchi according to the packet instructions. When the gnocchi has a few seconds to go, drop in the spinach, then drain the gnocchi and spinach together. Tip them both into the roasting tin, then mix everything together well, mashing the softened garlic. Spoon out on to warm serving plates, then crumble over the cheese to serve.

• Per serving 333 kcalories, protein 11g, carbohydrate 53g, fat 10g, saturated fat 4g, fibre 5g, sugar 8g, salt 1.76g

Come home to a bowl of this low-fat soup. Filled tortellini make a delicious change to ordinary pasta, and combined with the vegetables make this a high-fibre meal that gives three of your 5-a-day.

Hearty pasta soup

1 tbsp olive oil
2 carrots, chopped
1 large onion, finely chopped
1 litre/1¾ pints vegetable stock
400g can chopped tomatoes
with garlic
200g/8oz frozen mixed peas
and beans
250g pack fresh filled pasta (we used
tortellini with ricotta and spinach)
a handful of basil leaves, chopped
(optional)
freshly grated Parmesan and bread,
to serve (optional)

Takes 30 minutes • Serves 4

1 Heat the oil in a pan. Fry the carrots and onion for 5 minutes until starting to soften. Add the stock and tomatoes, then simmer for 10 minutes, adding the peas and beans after 5 minutes.
2 Once the vegetables are tender, stir in the pasta. Return to the boil and simmer for 2 minutes until the pasta is just cooked. Stir in the basil, if using. Season, then serve in bowls topped with a sprinkling of Parmesan and slices of bread.

• Per serving 286 kcalories, protein 11g, carbohydrate 44g, fat 9g, saturated fat 3g, fibre 6g, sugar 11g, salt 0.88g

Falafels are hugely popular in the Middle East – and no wonder, they're tasty, low in saturated fat and salt, and provide you with one of your 5-a-day. Here's a simple version straight from your storecupboard.

Falafel burgers

400g can chickpeas, rinsed and drained
1 small red onion, roughly chopped
1 garlic clove, chopped
a handful of flatleaf or curly parsley
1 tsp each ground cumin and coriander
½ tsp harissa paste or chilli powder
2 tbsp plain flour
2 tbsp sunflower oil
toasted pittas, 200g tub tomato salsa and green salad, to serve (optional)

Takes 15 minutes • Serves 4

1 Pat the chickpeas dry with kitchen paper. Tip into a food processor along with the onion, garlic, parsley, spices, flour and a little salt. Blend until fairly smooth, then shape into four patties with your hands.
2 Heat the oil in a non-stick frying pan, add the burgers, then quickly fry for 3 minutes on each side until lightly golden. Serve with toasted pittas, tomato salsa and a green salad.

• Per serving 161 kcalories, protein 6g, carbohydrate 18g, fat 8g, saturated fat 1g, fibre 3g, sugar 1g, salt 0.36g

Pile over hot couscous and enjoy a superhealthy meal high in fibre, low in fat, saturated fat and salt, and that contains four of your 5-a-day.

Vegetable tagine with chickpeas and raisins

2 tbsp olive oil
2 onions, chopped
½ tsp each ground cinnamon, coriander and cumin
2 large courgettes, cut into chunks
2 tomatoes, chopped
400g can chickpeas, drained and rinsed
4 tbsp raisins
425ml/¾ pint vegetable stock
300g/10oz frozen peas
chopped fresh coriander, to serve

Takes 30 minutes • Serves 4

1 Heat the oil in a pan, then fry the onions for 5 minutes until soft. Stir in the spices. Add the courgettes, tomatoes, chickpeas, raisins and stock, then bring to the boil. Cover and simmer for 10 minutes. Stir in the peas and cook for 5 minutes more. Sprinkle with coriander, to serve.

• Per serving 264 kcalories, protein 12g, carbohydrate 36g, fat 9g, saturated fat 1g, fibre 9g, sugar 19g, salt 0.52g

This low-fat dish has a sweet, slightly hot flavour that kids will love.

Noodles with stir-fried chilli veg

250g pack medium egg noodles
1 tbsp tomato purée
2 tbsp soy sauce
2 tbsp sweet chilli sauce
1 tbsp sunflower oil
a small piece of fresh root ginger, grated
300g pack Chinese-style stir-fry vegetables

Takes 15 minutes • Serves 4

1 Bring a pan of water to the boil. Add the noodles, bring back to the boil and cook for 4 minutes, then drain well. Mix the tomato purée, soy and chilli sauces in a small bowl with 150ml/¼ pint water.

2 Meanwhile, heat the oil in a large pan or wok, add the ginger and vegetables and stir fry for 2 minutes. Add the noodles and sauce to the wok, and cook for a further 2–3 minutes until everything is piping hot.

• Per serving 304 kcalories, protein 10g, carbohydrate 51g, fat 8g, saturated fat 1g, fibre 3g, sugar 6g, salt 2.2g

Trim the fat off steak and it can easily fit into a low-fat diet – especially when served with this delicious Middle Eastern-inspired salad.

Special steak with parsnip salad

sirloin steak (about 250g/9oz), trimmed of fat
2 parsnips, peeled and cut into strips or coarsely grated
4 dates, stoned and quartered lengthways
150g bag baby leaf salad with chard
a handful of mint leaves, to garnish

FOR THE DRESSING
3 tbsp low-fat crème fraîche
2 tsp horseradish sauce
a squeeze of fresh lemon juice

Takes 20 minutes • Serves 2

1 Heat a griddle pan until very hot, season the steak, then fry for 1½–2½ minutes each side for rare to medium and 4 minutes for well done. Remove from the pan and rest for 5 minutes, before thinly slicing.
2 Make the dressing by whisking the crème fraîche, horseradish sauce and lemon juice together in a large bowl. Tip in the parsnips and dates, then toss together with some seasoning. Divide the leaf salad between two plates with the parsnip salad on top. Lay the sliced beef over the salads and finish with a scattering of mint leaves.

• Per serving 474 kcalories, protein 35g, carbohydrate 60g, fat 11g, saturated fat 5g, fibre 10g, sugar 46g, salt 0.42g

Serve from the pot into bowls – this is a wonderful high-fibre meal for family and friends that's low in saturated fat and salt and also provides three of your 5-a-day. It's easily doubled if you're serving a large crowd.

Minted lamb and pea stew

350g/12oz lean lamb leg, cubed
1 tbsp plain flour, seasoned
1 tbsp sunflower oil
4 shallots, quartered
2 leeks, sliced
4 carrots, thickly sliced
400g/14oz potatoes, cut into large cubes
700ml/1¼ pints lamb or chicken stock
300g/10oz frozen peas
a handful of mint leaves, to serve

Takes 30 minutes • Serves 4

1 Toss the lamb in the flour. Heat half the oil in a large pan, then brown the lamb over a high heat for 2 minutes. Transfer to a plate, then add the rest of the oil, shallots, leeks, carrots and potatoes to the pan. Fry for a few minutes until starting to soften.
2 Pour over the stock, scraping up any meaty bits, then simmer for 10 minutes until the vegetables are almost cooked. Tip the lamb into the pan along with the peas, then simmer for 4 minutes or until the lamb is just cooked and the vegetables are tender. Scatter with mint leaves to serve.

• Per serving 357 kcalories, protein 28g, carbohydrate 37g, fat 12g, saturated fat 4g, fibre 10g, sugar 11g, salt 1.38g

Give these tasty low-fat bites a try with drinks, or serve as a starter to a healthy Indian meal. They're a good source of vitamin C and are low in fat, saturated fat and salt – so they'll keep everyone happy.

Prawn cakes with coriander sambal

3 slices white bread, halved
2 shallots, halved
1 garlic clove, crushed
400g/14oz raw peeled prawns
a generous grating of fresh nutmeg
1 large egg
2 tbsp sunflower oil, for frying

FOR THE SAMBAL
1 green pepper, seeded
1 green chilli, seeded
a knob fresh root ginger
2 garlic cloves
2 x 20g packs coriander
1 tsp caster sugar
2 tsp malt vinegar
juice of 1 small lemon

Takes 30 minutes • Serves 6

1 Put all the ingredients for the fishcakes, except the oil, in a food processor, with a little seasoning, and blitz until really well blended. Shape into 12–18 round patties, then chill, covered, in the fridge for up to 1 day or until ready to serve.
2 Wash the food processor, then blitz all the sambal ingredients together to make a bright green, wet paste. Season, put in a small serving bowl and chill.
3 When ready to serve, fry the fishcakes in the oil for a few minutes on each side until golden. They will be firm – like Thai fishcakes rather than those made with potato. Serve piled on to a platter with the bowl of sambal.

• Per serving 153 kcalories, protein 15g, carbohydrate 11g, fat 6g, saturated fat 1g, fibre 1g, sugar 2g, salt 0.61g

Start a smart dinner or family celebration with this seasonal soup. It's hearty and healthy, containing vitamin C and two of your 5-a-day, as well as being low in fat, saturated fat and salt.

Sherried squash soup

1 large onion, halved and sliced
2 tbsp olive oil
4 tbsp fino (dry) sherry
1kg/2lb 4oz butternut squash,
peeled, seeded and chopped
600ml/1 pint hot vegetable stock
croûtons and flatleaf
parsley sprigs, to serve (optional)

Takes 50 minutes • Serves 4
(easily doubled)

1 Fry the onion in the oil for 5 minutes until softened. Add the sherry and squash, and sizzle for 1–2 minutes. Pour in the stock, then cover and simmer for 20 minutes until the squash is tender when pierced with a knife.
2 Whiz in a food processor until smooth. When ready to eat, reheat until bubbling and serve in small portions topped with croûtons and a sprig of parsley.

• Per serving 183 kcalories, protein 4g, carbohydrate 26g, fat 6g, saturated fat 1g, fibre 5g, sugar 15g, salt 0.22g

For a relaxed vegetarian meal, you can't get much better than this. It's a superhealthy supper: high in fibre, a good source of iron and folic acid, and contains four of your 5-a-day.

Butter bean and squash crumble

350g/12oz dried butter beans, soaked overnight in cold water
4 tbsp olive oil
2 onions, chopped
4 garlic cloves, finely chopped
1–2 red chillies, seeded and finely chopped
700g jar passata
1 bouquet garni
425ml/¾ pint white wine
425ml/¾ pint vegetable stock
700g/1lb 9oz squash, peeled, seeded and cut into chunks

FOR THE CRUMBLE
50g/2oz breadcrumbs
25g/1oz walnuts, finely chopped
1 tbsp chopped fresh rosemary
4 tbsp chopped fresh parsley

Takes 2¾ hours • Serves 6

1 Rinse the beans and put them in a large pan with plenty of water to cover. Bring to the boil, reduce the heat and cook, partly covered, for about 1 hour until tender. Drain well.
2 Heat two tablespoons of oil in a pan, add the onions and fry for 10 minutes until lightly browned. Add the garlic, chillies, passata, bouquet garni, wine, stock, salt and pepper. Bring to the boil. Reduce the heat and simmer, uncovered, for 20 minutes. Add the squash and cook for a further 20 minutes.
3 Preheat the oven to 180°C/fan 160°C/ Gas 4. Stir the beans into the sauce, then transfer to a 2.5-litre/ 5 pint dish, or two smaller ones. Mix together all the crumble ingredients, plus the remaining two tablespoons of oil, then sprinkle it over the bean mixture. Bake for 30 minutes or until the topping is golden and crisp. Serve with bread and salad.

• Per serving 428 kcalories, protein 17g, carbohydrate 62g, fat 12g, saturated fat 2g, fibre 13g, sugar 18g, salt 0.93g

High in fibre, a good source of folic acid and vitamin C, plus low in saturated fat and salt, this Lancashire-hotpot-style dish is ideal for a winter gathering. Rabbit is a great low-fat choice.

Rabbit and mushroom hotpot

3 tbsp olive oil, plus extra for brushing
1 oven-ready rabbit, cut into legs, shoulders and 2 loins (discard the rib cage)
250g pack portabellini or other small flat mushrooms, thickly sliced
1kg/2lb 4oz large potatoes, thinly sliced
3 Spanish onions, halved and thinly sliced
1 tbsp chopped fresh rosemary
600ml/1 pint strongly flavoured chicken stock

Takes about 2¼ hours • Serves 4

1 Preheat the oven to 180°C/fan 160°C/Gas 4. Heat the oil in a deep flameproof and ovenproof casserole dish. Add the rabbit pieces, then fry briefly until browned. Remove to a plate, add the mushrooms to the dish and quickly stir fry them. Remove from dish and take it off the heat.

2 Layer half the potatoes into the dish, season with salt and pepper and layer with half the onions, the mushrooms and rosemary, then top with the rabbit. Repeat with the rest of the onions, mushrooms, rosemary, finishing with potatoes. Pour over the stock and brush the potatoes with oil.

3 Put the dish back on the heat and bring to the boil, then cover and put in the oven for 1¼ hours. Take off the lid, then return to the oven at 220°C/fan 200°C/Gas 7 for 30 minutes more to brown the top.

• Per serving 544 kcalories, protein 42g, carbohydrate 58g, fat 18g, saturated fat 4g, fibre 7g, sugar 11g, salt 1.04g

Blackberries are a perfect match for venison, a richly flavoured – and very low-fat – meat. This dish is also low in saturated fat and salt.

Pan-fried venison with blackberry sauce

1 tbsp olive oil
2 thick venison steaks or 4 medallions
1 tbsp balsamic vinegar
150ml/¼ pint good-quality beef stock
2 tbsp redcurrant jelly
1 garlic clove, crushed
85g/3oz fresh or frozen blackberries
mashed potato or celeriac and broccoli, to serve (optional)

Takes 25 minutes • Serves 4

1 Heat the oil in a frying pan and cook the venison for 5 minutes, then turn it over and cook it for 3–5 minutes more, depending on how rare you like it and the thickness of the meat. Lift the meat out of the pan and set aside to rest.
2 Add the balsamic vinegar to the pan, then pour in the stock, redcurrant jelly and garlic. Stir over quite a high heat to blend everything together, then add the blackberries and carry on cooking until they soften. Serve with the venison, mashed potato or celeriac and broccoli.

• Per serving 182 kcalories, protein 28g, carbohydrate 7g, fat 5g, saturated fat 1g, fibre 1g, sugar 7g, salt 0.24g

This pasta dish is a good source of iron and vitamin C, and provides one of your 5-a-day. Serve as a starter for six, if you like.

Stir-fried scallops and chorizo with spaghetti

12 scallops, with or without roe
500g pack fresh spaghetti
3 tbsp extra-virgin olive oil
¼ tsp dried chilli flakes
85g/3oz sliced chorizo, cut in small chunks
1 red and 1 orange pepper, halved, seeded and cut into big chunks
2 garlic cloves, finely sliced
1 small bunch flatleaf parsley, roughly chopped

Takes 25 minutes • Serves 4 (easily halved)

1 Trim the scallops, removing the small piece of white, opaque muscle. Detach the roes from the white meat, if they have them.

2 Cook the spaghetti according to the packet instructions, then drain and toss with olive oil, chilli and seasoning. Pile into a big, deep serving dish and keep warm.

3 Heat a frying pan and add the chorizo. Cook over a gentle heat until the fat starts to run, then turn up the heat, add the peppers and garlic, and stir fry for 3–4 minutes. Season and pile on top of the spaghetti.

4 Place the pan back on a high heat, add the scallops and roe, and fry for 1–2 minutes on each side until the white meat is lightly browned and the meat and roe are both firm. Add the scallops and parsley to the spaghetti, season and toss to mix. Serve in bowls, giving each person three scallops.

• Per serving 584 kcalories, protein 38g, carbohydrate 75g, fat 17g, saturated fat 3g, fibre 2g, sugar 7g, salt 0.93g

Treat someone special with this quick yet impressive dish, ready in just 20 minutes. Low in saturated fat and salt plus a good source of omega-3 and folic acid.

Salmon with tarragon hollandaise

1 tbsp olive oil
2 salmon fillets, skin on and scaled, about 140g/5oz each
125g pack asparagus tips, ends trimmed
2 bunches cherry tomatoes on the vine
1 tbsp chopped fresh tarragon
150ml/¼ pint ready-made hollandaise sauce, to serve

Takes 10 minutes • Serves 2

1 Preheat the oven to 200°C/fan 180°C/Gas 6. Heat the oil in an ovenproof pan over a high heat. Add the salmon, skin-side down, then cook for 5 minutes until the skin is crisp.
2 Add the asparagus and vine tomatoes to the pan, then place in the oven. Cook for 7–10 minutes until the salmon is just cooked through.
3 Add the tarragon to the hollandaise sauce and stir through. Drizzle over the salmon and vegetables and serve.

• Per serving 327 kcalories, protein 31g, carbohydrate 3g, fat 22g, saturated fat 4g, fibre 2g, sugar 3g, salt 0.18g

Serve this low-fat, low-salt dish with saffron rice and salad to make a simple, no-stress supper for friends.

Pan-fried pork with maple and mustard sauce

2 pork tenderloins, about 300g/
10oz each
1 tbsp plain flour
2 tbsp olive oil, plus extra (if needed)
1 red onion, thinly sliced
200ml/7fl oz vegetable stock
2 tbsp maple syrup
2 tbsp wholegrain mustard
juice of 1 lemon
a handful of parsley sprigs (optional),
to garnish

Takes 30 minutes • Serves 4

1 Cut the pork into 3cm/1in thick slices, season, then lightly coat in the flour. (The easiest way to do this is to put the flour and seasoning in a large food bag, add the pork and shake well.) Heat the oil in a large non-stick frying pan, then quickly fry the pork until it is browned all over. Remove to a plate and cover with foil.

2 Add the onion to the pan (with a touch more oil, if needed), fry for 5 minutes until light golden, add the stock, then bring to the boil. Boil hard for a couple of minutes to reduce the stock a little. Stir in the maple syrup, mustard and lemon juice, then bring back to the boil, stirring.

3 Return the pork to the pan and gently simmer for a further 3–4 minutes until it is cooked through. Sprinkle with parsley, if using.

• Per serving 327 kcalories, protein 35g, carbohydrate 11g, fat 16g, saturated fat 4g, fibre 1g, sugar 7g, salt 0.58g

Cooking the fish on top of the vegetables is a simple way to add flavour, and also stops it drying out during roasting. This fish dish is high in omega-3 and low in saturated fat and salt.

Baked sea bass with romesco sauce

4 red peppers, seeded and cut into large chunks
2 yellow peppers, seeded and cut into large chunks
5 large vine tomatoes, halved
1 large red onion, cut into wedges
4 large garlic cloves, unpeeled
4 tbsp olive oil, plus extra for drizzling
2 x 1kg/2lb 4oz whole line-caught sea bass, scaled and gutted
2 lemons, thinly sliced
2 large handfuls of fresh mixed herbs (such as rosemary and thyme)
2 tsp balsamic vinegar
50g/2oz whole hazelnuts, toasted

Takes about 1 hour • Serves 6

1 Preheat the oven to 220°C/fan 200°C/Gas 7. Tip the vegetables and garlic into a roasting tin. Season and toss with the oil. Roast for 20 minutes until starting to soften.
2 Pat the fish dry with kitchen paper, then slash the skin. Season the cavities, stuff with the lemons and half the herbs. Place on top of the vegetables, drizzle with oil, scatter with remaining herbs and roast for 20–25 minutes. When cooked, the flesh will feel firmer and the large back fins will pull away easily.
3 Lift the fish and half the vegetables on to a serving plate and cover with foil. Spoon the remaining vegetables and any roasting juices into a food processor. Add the vinegar and hazelnuts, blend until smooth, then check the seasoning. Lift the fish fillets off the bone and serve with the vegetables and sauce.

• Per serving 457 kcalories, protein 47g, carbohydrate 15g, fat 24g, saturated fat 3g, fibre 4g, sugar 13g, salt 0.43g

Stuffed pork loin is really simple but looks impressive. It cooks quickly too, making it perfect for a special supper when time is short. This recipe is a good source of iron but low in saturated fat and salt.

Apricot and cumin-stuffed pork

1 tsp cumin seeds
100g ready-to-eat apricots
400g/14oz lean pork fillet
1 tbsp sunflower oil
150ml/¼ pint Marsala, Madeira or port
1 fresh rosemary sprig
Potatoes and salad, to serve (optional)

Takes 25 minutes • Serves 2

1 Preheat the oven to 200°C/fan 180°C/Gas 6. Lightly toast the cumin in a frying pan. Tip into a blender with the apricots. Whiz until well chopped, but not smooth. Slice the pork in half horizontally, not cutting through it completely, and open it out like a book. Season. Spread the apricot mix along the centre. Fold the meat back over the stuffing.
2 Heat the oil in a pan and brown the meat all over for no more than 5 minutes. Lift the pork on to a roasting tin and cover loosely with foil. Roast for 10–15 minutes, or until lightly pink.
3 Heat the wine and rosemary in the frying pan and bring to the boil. Simmer for 5 minutes or until reduced to a sauce. Remove the meat from the oven and rest for 5 minutes before carving thickly. Pour any juices into the sauce, season to taste, then pour over the meat to serve.

• Per serving 428 kcalories, protein 46g, carbohydrate 24g, fat 14g, saturated fat 3g, fibre 3g, sugar 23g, salt 0.37g

This dish is a good source of iron, provides two of your 5-a-day and is low in saturated fat and salt. Serve it with cucumber raita and salad.

Baked aubergines stuffed with minced lamb

4 small, or 8 baby, aubergines
vegetable oil, for frying

FOR THE STUFFING
1 tbsp olive oil, plus extra for drizzling
1 large onion, finely chopped
4 garlic cloves, finely chopped
1–2 red or green chillies, seeded and finely chopped
1 tsp sugar
2 tbsp each currants and pine nuts
1 tbsp each ground cinnamon and garam masala
1 tsp turmeric
225g/8oz lean minced lamb
1 small bunch coriander leaves, finely chopped
2 tomatoes, sliced
lemon wedges, to serve

Takes 1 hour 10 minutes • Serves 4

1 Preheat the oven to 200°C/fan 180°C/Gas 6. Make the stuffing: heat the oil in a heavy pan, add the onion and cook gently for 5 minutes. Add the garlic and chillies, fry for 1 minute, add the sugar, currants and pine nuts and fry until the onions are golden. Stir in the spices, season, then set aside to cool.
2 Mix the lamb and coriander into the onion mix, then season. Heat a little vegetable oil in the heavy pan. Fry the aubergines until soft and golden brown all over, about 6–8 minutes. Remove to a baking dish. Using a sharp knife, slit each lengthways to form a pocket. Stuff the aubergines with the lamb mixture and place 2–3 slices of tomato on top of each one. Drizzle with oil and cover with foil.
3 Bake for 40 minutes, then uncover and bake for 10 minutes more or until the tomato has started to caramelize. Serve with lemon wedges for squeezing.

• Per serving 340 kcalories, protein 16g, carbohydrate 22g, fat 21g, saturated fat 4g, fibre 6g, sugar 15g, salt 0.14g

A classic Chinese way of serving fish – it's easy and is a good source of omega 3 and vitamin C, as well as being low in saturated fat and salt.

Sea bass with sizzled ginger, chilli and spring onions

6 fillets white fish, about 140g/5oz each, skin on and scaled
about 3 tbsp sunflower oil
a large knob of fresh ginger, peeled and shredded into matchsticks
3 garlic cloves, thinly sliced
3 fat fresh red chillies, seeded and thinly shredded
a bunch spring onions, shredded lengthways
1 tbsp soy sauce

Takes 25 minutes • Serves 6

1 Season the fish with salt and pepper, then slash the skin three times. Heat a heavy-based frying pan and add one tablespoon of oil. Once hot, fry the fish, skin-side down, for 5 minutes or until the skin is very crisp and golden. The fish will be almost cooked through. Turn the fish over, cook for another 30 seconds–1 minute, then transfer to a serving plate and keep warm. You'll need to fry the fish in two batches.

2 Heat the remaining oil, then fry the ginger, garlic and chillies for about 2 minutes until golden. Take off the heat and toss in the spring onions. Splash the fish with a little soy sauce and spoon over the contents of the pan. Serve with rice and your favourite stir-fried veg.

• Per serving 202 kcalories, protein 28g, carbohydrate 2g, fat 9g, saturated fat 1g, fibre none, sugar 1g, salt 0.26g

Crisp chocolate gives way to tender, slightly boozy pears in this gorgeously guilt-free dessert that's low in fat and contains no saturated fat.

Chocolate pear crisp

3 ripe pears, peeled and cored
juice of ½ lemon
1 tbsp light muscovado sugar
4 tsp Poire William liqueur or cognac
(optional)

FOR THE TOPPING
50g/2oz icing sugar
1 tbsp cocoa powder
25g/1oz ground almonds
1 egg white

Takes 50 minutes • Serves 4

1 Preheat the oven to 160°C/fan 140°C/ Gas 3. Chop the pears into small pieces and put them in a pan with the lemon juice and sugar. Bring to the boil, then cover and cook for 10 minutes. Uncover, then cook for 8–10 minutes more until the juices thicken up. Spoon into four 150ml/¼ pint ramekins and add one teaspoon of liqueur to each, if using.
2 For the topping, sift the icing sugar and cocoa into a bowl, then stir in the almonds. In a separate bowl, whisk the egg white until stiff, then fold into the dry ingredients. Spoon the mixture over the pears and shake the ramekins to level it. Bake for 20–25 minutes until the topping is firm to the touch. Serve warm or cold.

• Per serving 140 kcalories, protein 2g, carbohydrate 26g, fat 4g, saturated fat none, fibre 2g, sugar 25g, salt 0.03g

These zingy pancakes are perfect for Pancake Day or for entertaining at any other time of year. You'd never guess they're low in fat and saturated fat.

Quick crêpes Suzette

4 ready-made pancakes

FOR THE SAUCE
100g/4oz golden caster sugar
juice of 2 oranges and zest of 1
orange, plus extra wedges to
serve (optional)
a small knob of butter
half-fat crème fraîche, to serve
(optional)

Takes 20 minutes • Serves 4

1 Tip the sugar into a microwaveable bowl and stir in three tablespoons of orange juice to dampen. Microwave on High for 3–4 minutes until you have a bubbling caramel. Remove the bowl from the microwave (watch out – it will be very hot), then add the rest of juice, zest and butter. Return to the microwave and blast for 1 minute, stir, then cook for 1 more minute until the caramel has dissolved into the juice and you have a syrupy sauce. Set aside.

2 Heat the pancakes in the microwave according to the packet instructions. Serve each one folded into quarters with the sauce poured over, a spoonful of crème fraîche and orange wedges, if you like.

• Per serving 254 kcalories, protein 5g, carbohydrate 51g, fat 5g, saturated fat 3g, fibre 1g, sugar 31g, salt 0.66g

A superfruity summer dessert that's low in saturated fat and provides two of your 5-a-day. Add a splash of vodka or Cointreau, if you like.

Melon, orange and raspberry cups

1 medium melon, or a mix of two types, peeled and cut into small chunks
zest and juice of 1 orange
2 tbsp light brown soft sugar
150g punnet raspberries

Takes 15 minutes, plus standing
Serves 4

1 Tip the melon pieces into a large bowl. Splash over the orange juice and zest and sprinkle with the sugar. Mix well, then leave for 10 minutes or until the sugar dissolves.
2 Stir the raspberries through, then serve with ice cream or crème fraîche.

• Per serving 70 kcalories, protein 1g, carbohydrate 17g, fat 0.3g, saturated fat none, fibre 2g, sugar 17g, salt 0.05g

Cognac adds a delicious warmth and spiciness to this winter fruit medley that's low in fat and saturated fat, and tastes even better made ahead.

Dried fruits in cognac

85g/3oz light muscovado sugar
1 cinnamon stick
400g/14oz dried fruit (any combination of prunes, apricots, peaches and pears)
4 tbsp cognac
crème fraîche or ice cream, to serve (optional)

Takes 25 minutes • Serves 4–6

1 Tip the sugar into a pan and pour over 350ml/12fl oz boiling water. Add the cinnamon stick, broken in two, and stir to dissolve the sugar.
2 Add the fruits and cognac into the pan, then bring to the boil. Simmer, partly covered, for 15 minutes, then remove from the heat and leave to cool for a few minutes if serving warm, or chill if serving cold. Serve with some crème fraîche or ice cream.

• Per serving 322 kcalories, protein 3g, carbohydrate 72g, fat 1g, saturated fat 0.1g, fibre 6g, added sugar 24.8g, salt 0.08g

You can use any fruit and sorbet you like for this super quick, fat-free dessert idea that's special enough for summer entertaining.

Sorbet fizz

2 strawberries, sliced
2 scoops raspberry sorbet
100ml/3½fl oz sparkling elderflower drink

Takes 5 minutes • Serves 2

1 Arrange the strawberry slices in the bottom of two pretty, long-stemmed glasses, then top each with a scoop of raspberry sorbet. Pour over the elderflower drink and serve straight away.

• Per serving 136 kcalories, protein none, carbohydrate 35g, fat none, saturated fat none, fibre none, sugar 33g, salt 0.04g

A little chocolate goes a long way in these brilliantly easy puddings that are low in fat and saturated fat. Kids will love them, too.

Hot chocolate custard puds

2 tbsp sunflower oil, plus extra
for oiling
1 tbsp cocoa powder
100g/4oz self-raising flour
½ tsp bicarbonate of soda
50g/2oz golden caster sugar
100ml/3½fl oz skimmed milk
1 egg

FOR THE HOT CHOCOLATE
CUSTARD
2 × 150g pots low-fat custard
25g/1oz plain chocolate, chopped

Takes 20 minutes • Serves 6

1 Preheat the oven to 170°C/fan 150°C/Gas 3. Brush six holes of a muffin tin with a drop of oil. Sieve the cocoa into a large bowl, then add the rest of the dry ingredients. Stir to combine and make a well in the centre.
2 Beat the milk, egg and oil together in a jug, pour into the well in the dry ingredients, then stir quickly to make a batter. Spoon into the muffin tin and bake for 15 minutes or until risen and firm to the touch.
3 Heat the custard in the microwave according to the packet instructions, or in a pan, then tip in the chopped chocolate off the heat and stir until smooth. Turn the puddings into bowls and pour the custard over.

• Per serving 215 kcalories, protein 5g, carbohydrate 32g, fat 8g, saturated fat 2g, fibre 1g, sugar 17g, salt 0.59g

These glamorous little meringues are fat-free and only take 10 minutes to prepare.

Quick iced fruit meringues

250g bag frozen smoothie mix (we used banana and strawberry)
200g tub low-fat fromage frais
2 tbsp icing sugar, or to taste
100g punnet blueberries
1 or 2 bananas, sliced
4 small meringue nests

Takes 10 minutes, plus defrosting
Serves 4

1 Tip the smoothie mix into the bowl of a food processor 10 minutes before you want to use it. Spoon in two tablespoons of the fromage frais and the icing sugar, then whiz until you have a smooth and creamy sorbet-like mix. If your fruit is still a little too frozen, add one teaspoon of water and whiz again.
2 Stir in most of the blueberries and bananas, then scoop the mixture on top of the meringues. Top with the rest of the fromage frais and decorate with the remaining fruit. The fruit smoothie mix will make more than you need for four servings, but you can put the rest into a freezer container and freeze for up to 1 month.

• Per serving 175 kcalories, protein 5g, carbohydrate 40g, fat none, saturated fat none, fibre 2g, sugar 39g, salt 0.21g

Preserve the sweet flavour of juicy pomegranates in this
stunning, fat-free sorbet.

Pomegranate ice

450g/1lb caster sugar
8 pomegranates

Takes 40 minutes • Serves 8

1 Tip the sugar into a bowl and pour over
600ml/1 pint boiling water from a kettle. Stir
to dissolve, then set aside to cool.
2 Meanwhile, juice the pomegranates.
Squeeze and press the skin of seven of the
pomegranates vigorously to crush the seeds
inside. Hold the squashed fruit over a bowl,
slit the skin with a knife and the juice will pour
out. Mix the juice with the syrup and churn in
an ice-cream machine until set, then scoop
into a plastic container and freeze. If you
don't have an icecream machine, put into a
container in the freezer for 4 hours, mixing
the crytalized edges into the rest of the mix
every half hour, until smooth and slushy, then
freeze. Serve the sorbet in scoops, scattered
with a few seeds from the remaining fruit.

• Per serving 305 kcalories, protein 2g, carbohydrate
78g, fat none, saturated fat none, fibre 6g, sugar 78g,
salt 0.01g

Move over fruit crumbles – this delicious fruit pudding is a lot quicker to make and healthy too. It's a good source of iron and vitamin C, provides two of your 5-a-day and is low in saturated fat.

Gingery compote crunch

3 Bramley apples, peeled and thinly sliced
50g/2oz ready-to-eat apricots, roughly chopped
4 tbsp ginger jam, or more to taste
½ × 500g bag frozen forest fruits
200g/8oz crunchy oat cereal
50g/2oz pine nuts

Takes 20 minutes • Serves 4

1 Heat the grill to High. Lay the apple slices and apricots in a shallow, microwaveable baking dish, then add the jam and a splash of water. Cover with cling film and cook on High for 5 minutes or until the fruit starts to soften. Stir the frozen fruits through, re-cover and cook for another 3 minutes or until defrosted.
2 Mix together the cereal and pine nuts and spoon over the fruit mixture. Grill for 2 minutes until golden.

• Per serving 421 kcalories, protein 9g, carbohydrate 60g, fat 18g, saturated fat 2g, fibre 5g, sugar 38g, salt 0.08g

Finish a meal with a plate of this cooling fruit. Packed with vitamin C, this dessert is two of your 5-a-day, low in fat with no saturated fat.

Pineapple and pink grapefruit with mint sugar

1 medium pineapple
2 pink grapefruits
50g/2oz golden granulated sugar
a small bunch of fresh mint, leaves only

Takes 10 minutes • Serves 4

1 Use a sharp knife to top and tail the pineapple, then stand it upright on a chopping board. Carve away the skin and discard. Rest the pineapple on its side, then cut it into wafer-thin slices. Repeat with the grapefruits, cutting away the peel and pith, then cut into slices. Arrange the fruit on a serving platter, catching any juices, and set aside.

2 Using a pestle and mortar, pound the sugar and mint together until completely blended. Scatter the mint sugar over the fruit and serve with natural yogurt.

• Per serving 168 kcalories, protein 2g, carbohydrate 42g, fat 1g, saturated fat none, fibre 4g, sugar 41g, salt 0.02g

A warming, autumnal pud that's low in fat. If you don't have any amaretti biscuits, you could use gingernuts instead.

Easy baked pears with amaretti

4 ripe pears
100g/4oz ricotta
½ tsp ground cinnamon
4 tbsp clear honey, plus extra
to serve
8 crisp amaretti biscuits

Takes 25 minutes • Serves 4

1 Preheat the oven to 190°C/fan 170°C/ Gas 5. Cut each pear in half, then place them cut-side up on a large baking sheet. Use a teaspoon to scoop out the cores and make a dip in the centre of each. Dollop about one heaped teaspoon of ricotta into each dip, then sprinkle over the cinnamon and drizzle with a little honey.
2 Roast the pears in the oven for 10 minutes. Tip the biscuits into a food bag and use a rolling pin to crush them lightly. Remove the pears from the oven, then scatter the crumbs over each pear. Return to the oven for another 10 minutes or until the pears are soft and the biscuits are golden brown. Serve drizzled with honey.

• Per serving 198 kcalories, protein 4g, carbohydrate 39g, fat 4g, saturated fat 2g, fibre 4g, sugar 32g, salt 0.23g

This refreshing ice compliments strawberries beautifully.
Low in saturated fat, this granita is also a good source of vitamin C
and provides one of your 5-a-day.

Mango and vanilla granita

1 vanilla pod, split (optional)
140g/5oz caster sugar
2 large ripe mangoes
300g/10oz strawberries, sliced,
to serve

Takes 30 minutes, plus freezing
Serves 8

1 Tip the vanilla pod into a bowl with the sugar. Bring a kettle of water to the boil and pour 250ml/8fl oz water over the sugar. Stir until completely dissolved, then leave to cool.
2 Peel the mangoes and cut away all the flesh, then blitz it in a food processor until you have a smooth purée. Stir the purée into the syrup and fish out the vanilla pod. Freeze in a shallow container until slushy, then break up the ice into smaller crystals. Repeat the process three times until it's completely frozen and the texture of snow. Serve with sliced strawberries.

• Per serving 163 kcalories, protein 1g, carbohydrate 42g, fat none, saturated fat none, fibre 3g, sugar 41g, salt 0.02g

A stunning, fat-free dinner-party dessert, intensely flavoured with spices and red wine. Serve with a scoop of low-fat ice cream or crème fraîche, if you wish.

Poached pears in spiced red wine

1 vanilla pod
1 75cl bottle red wine
225g/8oz caster sugar
1 cinnamon stick, halved
1 fresh thyme sprig, plus extra sprigs to serve
6 pears, peeled, but kept whole and with stalk intact

Takes 40–50 minutes • Serves 6

1 Halve the vanilla pod lengthways, scrape out the seeds into a large pan, then add the wine, sugar, cinnamon and thyme. Cut each piece of pod into three long thin strips, add to the pan, then lower in the pears.

2 Poach the pears in a covered pan for 20–30 minutes, making sure they are submerged in the wine. The cooking time will very much depend on the ripeness of your pears – they should be tender all the way through when pierced with a cocktail stick. You can make these up to 2 days ahead and chill until needed.

3 Take the pears from the pan, then boil the liquid to reduce it by half so that it's syrupy. Serve each pear with the cooled syrup, a strip of vanilla, a piece of the cinnamon and a small, fresh thyme sprig.

• Per serving 235 kcalories, protein none, carbohydrate 51g, fat none, saturated fat none, fibre 2g, sugar 51g, salt 0.3g

Have your pud and eat it with this clever winter pudding – a perfect, low-fat alternative to apple pie.

Toffee apple pudding

1.5kg/3lb 5oz cooking apples, peeled, cored and sliced
zest and juice of 1 large lemon
4–5 tbsp caster sugar
175g/6oz light muscovado sugar
50g/2oz butter
2 tbsp golden syrup
10 thin slices white bread, crusts removed and halved
icing sugar, for dusting
custard, to serve (optional)

Takes 45 minutes • Serves 6

1 Preheat the oven to 190°C/fan 170°C/Gas 5. Butter an ovenproof dish. Put the apples into a pan, add the juice and lemon zest and five tablespoons of water. Boil, cover and cook for 7–10 minutes until very soft. Stir in the sugar and cook, uncovered, for a few minutes until the mixture is thick and pulpy.

2 Put the muscovado sugar, butter, golden syrup and three tablespoons water into a pan. Bring to the boil, stirring as the sugar dissolves. Boil for 1–2 minutes until slightly syrupy and toffee-coloured.

3 Using a fork, dip half the bread pieces into the toffee, one at a time. Use them to line the prepared dish. Spoon the apple over the bread. Dip the rest of the bread in the toffee and use to cover the apple, overlapping slightly. Bake for 20–25 minutes until golden. Cool slightly before serving.

• Per serving 397 kcalories, protein 4g, carbohydrate 83g, fat 8g, saturated fat 5g, fibre 3g, sugar 63g, salt 0.72g

This delicate, fat-free dessert is pure summer in a bowl. Serve with a scoop of frozen yogurt or vanilla sorbet.

Baked peaches with rosewater

6 ripe peaches, halved and stoned
juice of 1 or 2 large oranges
2 tbsp rosewater
100g/4oz caster sugar
2 cinnamon sticks, broken

Takes 30 minutes • Serves 6

1 Preheat the oven to 220°C/fan 200°C/ Gas 7. Arrange the peaches cut-side up in a large, shallow heatproof dish so they fit quite snugly. Mix together the orange juice and rosewater, pour over the peaches, then scatter generously with the sugar. If you're using a large dish, the orange juice will evaporate more quickly, in which case use the juice from two oranges instead of one.
2 Add the cinnamon and bake for 20 minutes or until the peaches are tender. Alternatively, wrap the peaches in a big foil parcel and cook on the barbecue. Serve warm or chilled.

• Per serving 106 kcalories, protein 1g, carbohydrate 27g, fat none, saturated fat none, fibre 2g, sugar 27g, salt 0.01g

This delicious and different sorbet is fat free, low in salt and contains no saturated fat. It looks wonderful served in shot or cocktail glasses.

Redcurrant sorbet

450g/1lb redcurrants, plus extra
for decoration
2 tbsp elderflower cordial
140g/5oz golden caster sugar

Takes 40 minutes, plus freezing
Makes 4 small portions

1 Remove the redcurrants from their stems, wash and put in a pan with two tablespoons of water. Bring to the boil, lower the heat, cover and simmer for 5 minutes until softened. Push through a sieve to make a purée. Stir in the elderflower cordial and set to one side to cool.
2 Put the caster sugar in a pan with 300ml/½ pint water and leave over a low heat for 5 minutes until the sugar dissolves. Raise the heat and boil for 10 minutes.
3 Tip the redcurrant mixture into the syrup and mix. Return to the boil, turn down and simmer for 2 minutes. Cool, pour into a container and freeze for 3–4 hours until frozen. Scoop into glasses and top with redcurrants.

• Per serving 178 kcalories, protein 1g, carbohydrate 46g, fat none, saturated fat none, fibre 4g, added sugar 41g, salt 0.01g

Index

213   Index

Picture credits and recipe credits

BBC *Good Food* magazine and BBC Books would like to thank the following people for providing photos. While every effort has been made to trace and acknowledge all photographers, we should like to apologize should there be any errors or omissions.

Marie-Louise Avery p205; Peter Cassidy p13, p179, p184; Jean Cazals p173, p203, p211; Gareth Morgans p6, p11, p19, p21, p23, p25, p31, p33, p37, p39, p45, p49, p53, p55, p57, p61, p71, p75, p99, p119, p121, p123, p131, p133, p135, p137, p139, p143, p145, p147, p149, p167, p169, p175, p189, p191, p193, p197, p199; David Munns p27, p29, p35, p59, p95, p115, p117, p159, p171, p187, p207, p209; Myles New p15, p63, p77, p81, p101, p103, p109, p125, p127, p129, p151, p155, p183; Lis Parsons p41, p51, p79, p91, p111, p161; Michael Paul p47; Craig Robertson p17, p67, p153; Brett Stevens p201; Roger Stowell p73, p113, p181; Debbie Treloar p97; Simon Walton p43, p69, p141; Philip Webb p93, p107, p157, p163, p165, p177, p195;

Kate Whitaker p89, p105

All the recipes in this book were created by the editorial team at *Good Food* and by regular contributors to the magazine.